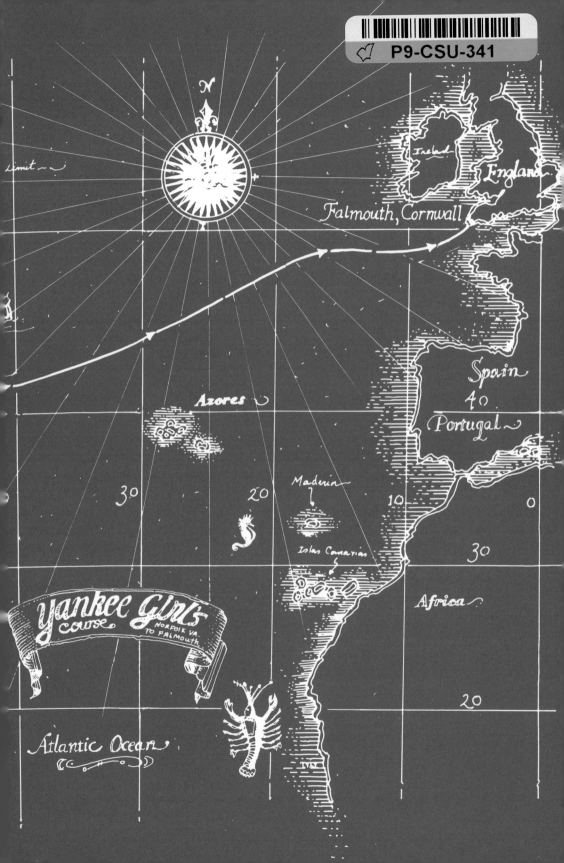

YANKEE GIRL AT DAWN
by Jerome F. Ryan

YANKEE GIRL AT DAWN
by Jerome F. Ryan

**From a signed and numbered
Limited Edition print,
autographed by Gerry Spiess.**

ALONE AGAINST
THE ATLANTIC

ALONE AGAINST THE ATLANTIC

GERRY SPIESS

with Marlin Bree

 CONTROL DATA PUBLISHING
a Control Data Company

Minneapolis, Minnesota
1981

ALONE AGAINST THE ATLANTIC

by Gerry Spiess
with Marlin Bree

Editor: Pamela Espeland
Design: Koechel/Peterson Design
Illustrator: Aldo Abelleira
Glossary: Ann Waters

Library of Congress Cataloging in Publication Data
Spiess, Gerald F., 1940-
Alone against the Atlantic.
1. Spiess, Gerald F., 1940-   . 2. Yankee Girl (ship) 3. North Atlantic
Ocean. 4. Travelers—United States—Biography. I. Bree, Marlin,
1933-   . II. Title.
G470.s66   910'.09163   81-9722
ISBN 0-89893-506-7   AACR2

Dedication

To those who dream—
and live their dreams.

Acknowledgments

Although I sailed alone,
I carried with me the hopes
and wishes of many others.
Their loving support
buoyed my spirits and gave me strength
in my most desperate hours.
Those who believed in me
can never know how large a role they played
in the realization of my dream.

Contents

I

Storm Over White Bear

July 1978

Purple clouds towered over the western horizon as I hurried toward White Bear Lake. I recognized their ominous formation: *cumulonimbus mammas.* Trouble clouds. Out of them could come the bane of all inland sailors—a tornado.

The air was heavy with the coming storm, and I shivered as I reached the dock at Tally's Anchor Inn. White Bear Lake, usually a serene, silvery-blue sailor's paradise, was now a leaden shade of gray. No multi-hued mallards bobbed among its rows of sailboats; no swallows flew overhead. The lake looked dead.

At the water's edge, two teenage boys were hastily dragging

Tally's rental fishing boats out of the lake and onto the shore. They stopped for a moment to watch a lone fisherman race his boat—its outboard motor whining at full throttle, its bow lifted high into the air—toward the dock.

"That's the last of them," said one of the boys, sounding relieved.

"All right, you two, don't just stand there," barked a gruff female voice from behind us. "Get those boats put away!" The boys jumped, and so did I.

I turned around. The voice belonged to Millie, Tally's manager, bait seller, and all-around boss. She frowned when she saw me. "Don't you know there's a tornado watch on tonight?" she asked accusingly.

"Sure," I replied. "That's why I'm here. It's a good night for me to do some real testing."

"Not if there's a tornado on the way," Millie snapped. Her tone caught me by surprise. Millie usually joked about my sailing habits, referring to me as White Bear's resident "foul-weather sailor." She had often stood on shore and watched as I headed out onto the lake while other sailors were hurrying in. Normally she just shook her head in mock disgust—but tonight she was not amused.

"We're closing," Millie said sternly. "The boys won't be around to help you." I could tell she hoped that her news would keep me from going out on the lake. My boat was moored about 175 feet from the dock, and I needed one of Millie's rental rowboats to reach it. Usually a dockboy shuttled me to and from my mooring, but tonight, it appeared, I would be on my own.

"That's okay," I said. "I'll just tie the rowboat to the mooring."

"But you'll be all alone," she protested.

"My boat was built for bad weather," I answered, trying to reassure her. The wind had loosened my glasses, and with one finger I pushed them back against my face.

Millie studied the sky. "At least you won't be able to stay

out very long," she told me. Then, nodding to herself, she turned abruptly and marched down the long dock toward shelter.

I had won the battle with Millie, but I had no time to waste in enjoying my little victory. As I glanced across the bay at Johnson's Boat Works, I could see other sailors dashing for their cars, hastily-gathered sails flapping loosely in their arms. I would be alone on the lake with the storm.

The last of Millie's boats, the one carrying the fisherman, bumped into the dock. As the fisherman climbed out, I clambered in, stepping over a pile of empty beer cans in the bilge. One of the dockboys helped me lift off the boat's motor, which I wouldn't be needing for my short trip to the mooring. Then I threw my weight hard against the oars and, fighting the wind, headed out toward my own boat.

A stubby little craft only ten feet long, *Yankee Girl* lay tethered at the next-to-the-last buoy. Because of her size, I often had to endure the teasing of other sailors. I was used to comments like, "Where's the rest of it?" and "Does that thing really sail?" Yet *Yankee Girl* remained, in my eyes at least, the most beautiful boat in the world. I knew every inch of her—from the curve in her stem to the rise of her chine, from the tip of her mast to the edge of her blue waterline. I had designed her, built her, rigged her, tested her, felt her every motion in wind and water.

I knew the secret she carried: my dream of a solo Atlantic crossing.

Now, in the rising wind, her bow line tugging against the mooring, she seemed anxious to get underway. I tied the rowboat to the mooring and then scrutinized the western horizon once more. It looked bad. The purple-black wall of clouds was closing in fast, swallowing the last of the sun's rays. If I didn't set sail almost immediately, I would be stranded on the mooring, for it would soon be too dangerous to row back to shore and too difficult to hoist *Yankee Girl*'s sails.

As I climbed aboard, *Yankee Girl*'s hull heeled slightly under my weight. Within moments I had slipped her sail covers off, unlocked the hatch, and dropped inside the cabin where the strong, pleasant aromas of plywood, paint, and beef jerky greeted me. Once inside the quiet, familiar hull, I rested briefly and listened to the developing storm. One moment the wind was nearly still; the next it tugged and whistled in the rigging.

It was time to get some sea room. I reached down into the footwell to pull out my four-horsepower Evinrude outboard motor. Hefting its 40 pounds over the transom, I secured the outboard tightly to its aluminum bracket so it couldn't shake loose. My safety depended on that motor. Then I crouched down on the berth and wormed my way into the forepeak to screw the plastic, mushroom-shaped ventilator shut. Now the main hatch behind me was the only opening on *Yankee Girl* that could let in water.

Lifting a locker cover on a floorboard, I peered into *Yankee Girl*'s white bilge. It was filled with ballast—720 pounds of water in plastic jugs. In the past the caps on the jugs had sometimes come loose, causing the bilge to slosh with water. At the moment, though, everything looked fine.

With the boat secure and dry inside, I was almost ready to cast off. I only needed to check the engine. After closing the choke, I made a few slow pulls on the starting cord to get the gas up. Then I yanked the cord hard. Immediately the Evinrude sputtered to life. I spun the motor around and *Yankee Girl* began to back up obediently.

After giving the motor a few seconds to warm up, I shut it off, and *Yankee Girl* and I drifted back toward the mooring. Meanwhile an eerie calm had settled over White Bear; it was time to set *Yankee Girl* free. I crawled to her bow, untied the mooring rope, and scrambled back toward the stern. Then I started the motor again and gently guided the boat out toward the center of the lake. As soon as we were clear of the shore and buoys, I turned off the motor and hoisted *Yankee Girl*'s sails.

Suddenly the first unstable gust of gale-force wind hit us

broadside, and *Yankee Girl* reeled under the blow. Gritting my teeth, I prepared for the worst. I knew I could not turn back now, for I had something to prove—if only to myself.

Advance winds from the onrushing storm pushed against *Yankee Girl*'s white dacron sails until they were as stiff as iron. Her nylon sail slugs rattled in the mast slot. She had come to life and was literally humming along through the gray water, raising a frothy bone of foam at her bow. I braced my knee against her short tiller to counterbalance the rudder's bite on the surging waves beneath her keel.

Manitou Island lay off to port and Bellaire Point, with its underwater rocks, was off to starboard. Ahead stretched open water. There, I reasoned, *Yankee Girl* would be safe when the full storm hit, for as long as she had sufficient water under her keel and room to maneuver she could take anything the weather threw at her.

Beginning to enjoy the ride, I settled back on my special "tiller seat," a sort of saddle I had connected to the transom's top just inches above the stubby tiller. From there I had a splendid view of sails, sky, and water. The arrangement was perfect for me, but anyone who saw me perched on top of my invention would have had a good laugh. My boat was so small that part of my posterior hung out over the edge.

As the first drops of rain splattered loudly on *Yankee Girl*'s cabin top, the surface of the lake began to ripple into dark catspaws. I reached for my worn *Minnesota Twins* baseball cap and jammed it on my head; its long bill would help to keep water off of my face. Over the cap I pulled the hood of my foul-weather jacket.

The test had begun. My goal was really very simple: All I wanted to do was to keep *Yankee Girl*'s sails up for as long as I could. I hoped to learn two things from my experience. First, I needed to find out how much wind my boat could take before heeling over on her beam ends. Second—and most important—I had to know whether I had the strength to pull her sails down during a major storm. Already, under this gale's increasing fury, *Yankee Girl*'s sails were becoming steel-tight. If conditions worsened, I wondered, would I be able to get the sails down before the boat capsized or her rig was damaged?

Buffeted on all sides, *Yankee Girl* began to heel alarmingly. Water rushed over her port rail. She was in danger; the wind was too strong. I reached for the mainsheet, which was vibrating violently in its cleat, and yanked it out. Immediately *Yankee Girl* fought her way upright and surged forward at full speed.

From now on, I knew, I would not be able to relax for even a moment. Bracing my knee against the tiller, I sailed with one hand on the mainsheet, ready to let go in an instant, and the other tightly gripping the windward rail for balance.

I glanced at *Yankee Girl*'s aluminum mast to see whether it was vibrating. That—or a humming sound—would signal that it was being forced out of its column by the wind. There was something else I was worried about: If the pressure kept up, the mast could snap in two and come crashing down on me, shrouds, sails, and all. This had happened to me once before on a 15-foot trimaran I had owned years ago. Under tremendous loading from the wind, the trimaran's mast had snapped so fast I hadn't even seen it go. One moment it had been up; the next it had been a tangle of metal and wire. I had been lucky—the mast could have punched through the cabin top and penetrated the hull like a metal spear.

Yankee Girl's mast was in good shape, but the wind was playing games with her and she was heeling sharply. The more she leaned, the more bottom she exposed to the wind. An especially strong blast at the right moment could capsize her.

Never before had *Yankee Girl* faced such a powerful storm. There was a chance that this test would prove to be more than I had bargained for—or would be able to withstand. Cautiously I headed the boat's bow directly into the wind. Suddenly freed of the tremendous pressure that had been on them, *Yankee Girl*'s sails cracked with the sound of whips above my head. I lashed the tiller. It was time to douse the sails—if I could. I had to bring them down.

I wrenched the halyard free and waited for the sail to rattle down, but nothing happened. The wind had jammed the sail in its slot. In order to loosen it I would have to leave the protection of the cabin and go out on deck. Too late I remembered that I had foolishly left my safety harness at home.

I had no choice, though; with or without my harness, I would have to bring that sail down. I pulled myself forward and up out of the cabin. The wind caught at my clothing and did its best to push me into the wind-whipped water. Above me swung the heavy wooden boom, missing my head by inches.

With my right foot, I slid the cabin's hatch closed. At a time like this, *Yankee Girl* couldn't afford to take on any water. The wind screamed around me; the rain was falling so heavily that I could barely see beyond *Yankee Girl*'s blunt bow. Clinging with one hand to the mast, I reached high and grabbed a handful of slippery dacron. With a yank I pulled the sail down.

I had accomplished that much, but the task I dreaded most still lay ahead: the jib had to be secured. I inched forward slowly on my knees. Meanwhile, under my weight, the boat plunged into the waves. Water surged up and over my legs, wetting me to the waist.

As the boat fought to regain her balance, I was thrown against the forestay and the sharp stainless-steel wire cut into my collarbone. Desperately I caught the wire in the crook of one arm to keep from being thrown back against the mast. Then, with my free hand, I gathered in the jib and jammed it under the shock cord.

My work done, I quickly scrambled back to the cabin, wrenched open the hatch, and jumped below. After slamming the hatch shut above me, I slumped down in the tiny space and sighed in relief. Never again, I promised myself, would I be caught in a storm without my safety harness.

I needed power to maintain my position in the center of the lake or the wind would drive me back to shore. Although the Evinrude was soaked by now, one quick tug brought it back to life. I smiled gratefully. Unlashing the tiller, I headed *Yankee Girl* directly into the jaws of the wind. We seemed to be blowing backwards, so I turned the throttle up to three-quarters power. Even with the added boost *Yankee Girl* made barely enough speed to give us steerageway. Still, she was holding her own.

With the hatch closed and me inside the cabin, protected from the wind and rain, I was relatively comfortable. A second—and unplanned-for—part of the test was just beginning, however. Crouched down in *Yankee Girl*'s belly, I could not see in front of her to what lay ahead; nor could I tell precisely where we were going. I could only estimate my position, hold my compass course, and hope for the best.

"So far, so good," I told myself. "We'll just sit here until the storm ends."

All things considered, I was pretty satisfied. We were in the midst of the worst weather *Yankee Girl* had ever experienced, and she was coming through with flying colors. I had learned a lot about her tonight: I knew now that she could stand up to heavy winds and maneuver in them. Even more important, though, was my discovery that I could depend on her. In spite of the ferocity of the storm, I was in no real danger—as long as I held my heading, kept the motor running, and maintained my mid-lake position. That didn't seem like too much to ask.

I glanced at my waterproof watch: it was 6:37 P.M. By now my wife Sally would be home from work. I had left her a note telling her that I'd gone sailing and letting her know that she didn't have to wait for me on shore; I was glad I'd thought to do so. Outside was no place for anyone to be—not on a night like this.

Through the persistent crackle of static emanating from her car radio, Sally could hear the newscaster's warning: *tornado watch*. She wished that she had left work earlier. It was a long drive from her office in Edina, a southern suburb of Minneapolis, to the home she shared with Gerry in White Bear Lake, a northern suburb of St. Paul.

At 5:45 P.M. she pulled into the driveway of their three-bedroom rambler, located only a few blocks from the lake. She was relieved to finally be home, for it had been a tiring day. Lately her workload as a manager for a computer consulting firm had been heavier then usual. As she climbed wearily out of her car, she turned to get a quick glimpse of the western horizon. Dark, low-hanging clouds crowded the sky. The storm was very close.

She didn't care, though, now that she was home. Tonight she and Gerry would sit snugly in their living room, listening to the radio from time to time in case the tornado watch became an alert and the possibility of a tornado turned into a sighting.

She was surprised to find the front door locked.

"Hello!" she called out as she opened the door with her key. No response. She walked into the kitchen and looked around. Gerry, in his meticulous way, had washed the breakfast dishes by hand before putting them into the dishwasher. She was still smiling about that when she saw the note on the table:

> *Gone sailing. Probably be back*
> *late, don't wait for me.*
> > *Love, Ger.*

Sally sighed. The long day was about to get longer. She glanced at her watch: it was now 5:48 P.M. Perhaps Gerry hadn't heard the news about the tornado watch.

Sally hurried into the master bedroom and changed into her jeans. She would go down to the mooring, she decided, and tell Gerry about the weather bureau's warning. Then she could help him secure *Yankee Girl* against the coming storm. That would be better than waiting around the house for him to return.

As she passed the refrigerator on her way out the door, she grabbed a couple of Red Delicious apples, Gerry's favorite snack. She knew her husband of sixteen years; he ate little but often. Another idea came to her: If it did start to rain, Gerry might need some dry clothes. She backtracked to the bedroom.

By the time Sally was on her way to Tally's, the storm had turned day into dusk. She switched on her headlights and then, as the first raindrops hit, her windshield wipers. Above her, tree limbs bent and swayed; the wind was rising fast. One sudden gust nearly shoved her into the other lane.

At Tally's, she jumped out of her car and slammed the door shut.

"That's odd," she thought, bracing herself against the wind as she approached the boathouse. "Millie hasn't turned on the lights yet."

Sally walked up to a window and peered inside. All was dark. With mounting concern, she raced around the building to the hill beside the lake. She took the steep steps to the water's edge two at a time.

Empty boats bobbed up and down on the cold, gray water. Gerry—and *Yankee Girl*—were nowhere to be seen.

Suddenly afraid, Sally turned away from the lake and ran up the dock to her car.

I headed deeper into the teeth of the storm. Gale-force winds shrieked in the rigging. Rain thundered on the cabin top and reverberated through *Yankee Girl*'s plywood hull. Over all that noise, I could barely hear the rasp of the outboard motor.

My eyes hurt from the strain of following the swings of the compass card. The storm was worsening; wind gusts driving the rain and scud were approaching the 60-mile-an-hour range. I was afraid to let *Yankee Girl* fall off the wind too much; the pressure on her rig was tremendous, but it pushed her down into the water and helped to steady her. We plowed on through the black water.

Lightning crackled around me, illuminating the rain-and-wind-scoured sky. All that electricity, I knew, was looking for a route into the water. That route could be me, for *Yankee Girl*'s aluminum mast offered the heavens a perfect lightning rod. I was glad that her mast tip was connected by a heavy wire to a six-inch-square copper plate on her bottom. That plate, I hoped, would protect us both in the event of a strike.

Another thought caused me to shift uneasily. In the bilge, in addition to the water jugs, I had stowed almost 300 pounds of steel weights and lead castings for ballast. It was possible that one of those weights or castings had snapped a lightning connector while I was shoving them around to make them fit into the tiny space. If that had happened, then lightning could sizzle downward, jump the wire, and burn a hole right through the bottom of the boat. . . .

I shook my head. I *had* to think positively, act positively. I had to keep trusting in *Yankee Girl*—in myself, really, for *Yankee Girl* was very much a part of me. I had designed her, built her, and cared for her. She was a spatial extension of my own mind. If I ever lost confidence in her, it would be the same as losing confidence in myself.

Suddenly I sat upright. Across the water, borne by the wind, drifted the chilling wail of a siren. I knew that sound: it came from White Bear Lake's rescue squad. Someone had been hurt or was in danger. I thought of Sally—of her sitting at home, hearing the siren, and wondering whether it was meant for me. But there was nothing I could do to allay her fears; I had no way of contacting her. All I could do was to sit tight in *Yankee Girl*'s cabin and ride out the storm.

As I peered into the misty gloom, I wondered what trials were still to come.

Sally maneuvered her car in a zigzag path down the road that wound beside the lake. By this time the rain was falling in thick sheets, turning the pavement into a river of hubcap-deep water. At one point Sally was forced to swerve to the left, narrowly missing a broken tree branch that hung down over the road. She pulled off at Bellaire Beach.

"Where *is* he?" she asked aloud, scanning the water. Even on bright her headlights were useless as spotlights; they illuminated the lake for only a few yards in front of her. Clutching her rainwear about her, she left the car and ran down to the beach.

No Gerry. No *Yankee Girl*. Not even a glimmer of her cabin lights.

Sally returned to her car. She would simply have to keep circling the lake until she found him. Her mind buzzed with disconcerting questions. What if the high winds had overpowered the tiny boat? What if *Yankee Girl* was somewhere in the middle of White Bear at this very moment—bottom-up with Gerry trapped inside her?

No, she told herself sternly, *that could never happen.* Gerry had designed *Yankee Girl* to be virtually uncapsizeable. Even so, she could not completely banish the thought from her mind. This was, after all, the worst storm in years. The tornado watch was still in effect; the weather announcer was reporting winds of over 60 miles per hour. What could winds like those do to a sailboat the size of *Yankee Girl?*

By now Sally had driven nearly three-quarters of the way around the lake—past the peninsula along the eastern shore, past the fashionable suburb of Dellwood, past the White Bear Yacht Club, past the public park at the northeastern end. She had stopped several times to run down to the water's edge and look for boats. And each time she had returned to her car, disappointed and increasingly fearful.

Finally Sally turned off the road and stopped by a wooden bridge that led across the water to Manitou Island. The island had sheltered small boats in the past; maybe Gerry was waiting here for the storm to subside. She climbed out of her car and trudged through the darkness toward the beach.

She stopped dead, stunned by what she saw. Three capsized boats had broken loose from their moorings and washed up on the beach. She looked more closely: *Yankee Girl* was not among them.

Drenched to the skin, Sally got back into her car for one more turn around the lake. But when she reached Tally's she decided to go no further. The worst of the storm was over, and the howling winds had given way to the hiss of a steady drizzle. Exhausted and light-headed—she had eaten nothing since breakfast—she started down the slippery steps leading to the dock. She would wait there for Gerry. Wait and hope. There was nothing else she could do.

Halfway down the steps, Sally clapped her hand to her mouth in shock.

With her white mast reaching down toward the water and her blue bottom turned upward, *Yankee Girl* lay capsized in the dark water along the south dock.

Too frightened to move, Sally stood there for a second, staring at the small boat driven helplessly against the dock. Then she rushed toward it.

The wind had diminished to a whisper. The lake, which so recently had shown its full strength, now displayed only a few gentle ripples on its surface. *Yankee Girl* ghosted toward shore under the outboard's power. The storm—and the test—were over. Both *Yankee Girl* and I had passed.

As I neared land, I saw two stranded boats which had been torn from their moorings and tossed into the bushes along the beach. Higher up the hill, Tally's was dark. I decided to steer *Yankee Girl* to the dock rather than to her mooring. Millie didn't like sailboats at the dock; I had often heard her complain, in no uncertain terms, "They take up too much space with all their paraphernalia." But tonight neither she nor anyone else was around to watch. It was the perfect time and place to find out one more thing about my *Yankee Girl*.

With a light bump, we arrived at the dock. I stepped ashore carefully, for it was difficult to tell where to tread. Following the storm, the lake's water level had risen until now it was almost even with the top of the dock.

I needed to know how much force it would take to knock *Yankee Girl* on her beam ends or even roll her 360 degrees. With her five-and-a-half-foot beam, she was buoyant enough to bob around like a cork in most weather conditions. But what if she were suddenly hit by a violent squall with all her sails standing? Would she be able to right herself then? I decided to do my best to discover the answer.

Stretching out from the dock, I reached up high on *Yankee Girl*'s port shroud. At first the ⅛-inch stainless-steel wire leading to the top of her mast slipped through my hand, but I soon managed to get a firm grip. Pulling hard on the shroud wire, I tried to bring *Yankee Girl* down on her beam. But, like an eager puppy, she only came closer toward me, nudging her painted side against the dock.

I *had* to find out what her righting moment was. I stood on top of her cabin and jumped down onto her deck. *Yankee Girl* heeled under my weight and then stubbornly rolled right back up again.

I climbed onto her cabin top and leaned against a shroud to rest and think. I had almost forgotten how fresh and still the lake became after a storm; breathing deeply, I relaxed for the first time that night.

I was glad to be alone. No one was here to observe me; for once, no one would question or laugh at what I was doing. On the other hand, no one had seen me come out of the storm or witnessed *Yankee Girl*'s flawless performance. Tomorrow the people who scoffed at my tiny boat would see her tethered quietly to her mooring. Her small triumph would remain a secret.

I cut short my reverie; it was time to return to the business at hand. It was late, and I wanted to get home to Sally.

Stretching my arms upward again, I reached as high as I could on the port shroud. Grasping it firmly, I jumped and swung like Tarzan toward the dock. As soon as my feet touched down, I grabbed for *Yankee Girl*'s mast tip and pulled on it with all my weight until her spar was horizontal with the lake's surface.

She was down. Her bottom jutted out of the water; her port side was partially submerged. Immediately she began to struggle upward. I looked about for a way to hold her in this position so I could inspect her more closely, but I didn't dare move. The thousand pounds of ballast deep in her bilge were trying to force the mast back into the air—and me with it. I was on one end of a teeter-totter with an 1,800-pound boat on the other.

I let *Yankee Girl* ease up slightly. Then I locked my fingers together over her mast tip and hung there. I had to find a way to keep her down. I looked about for a piece of rope, or perhaps a halyard, that I could hook under one of the planks in the dock.

Suddenly I felt more than saw something move on the steps leading up the hill to Tally's. I pulled myself up a few inches and peered into the dim light. I could barely make out the shape coming down the steps—but I knew it was Sally.

Why was she here? Had something happened?

Puzzled, I eased myself up even more. Then the realization

hit me: all Sally could see was *Yankee Girl*'s upturned bottom.

"Sal, I'm here!" I shouted, still hanging on to the mast.

Sally ran down the remaining steps and raced across the dock. As soon as she reached me, she threw her arms around my neck.

All three of us—Sally, *Yankee Girl*, and I—bumped down on the dock, for I refused to let go of that mast.

"What on earth happened?" Sally asked, her voice trembling.

"I've been doing some testing," I answered. "I wanted to get *Yankee Girl* down to check her righting ability."

Sally pulled away from me. "I thought she had capsized and washed up on the dock," she said. "I was *so* worried!"

Abruptly I released the mast. It soared into the murky sky as *Yankee Girl* righted herself.

I put my arms around Sally and held her tight. She was soaked to the skin.

"I drove all around the lake looking for you," she said. "Didn't you hear the tornado warnings?"

"I was watching the sky the whole time," I said gently. "I'm sorry."

I knew an apology wasn't enough. While I had been waiting out the storm in *Yankee Girl*'s cabin, Sally had been driving through it, searching for me.

I could see that she was rapidly becoming more upset. I had to get her back to reality and help her put her fears to rest. In a flash I knew what to do: I would turn her attention to *Yankee Girl*.

"Want to give me a hand?" I asked.

"What?"

"Will you help me hold her down?"

I stood up and pulled Sally to her feet. She followed me hesitantly as I stepped over to the boat. *Yankee Girl* bobbed quietly in the water, her tiny portholes dimly illuminated by the soft glow of the cabin lights.

Sally was silent for a moment.

"Won't the water come in through the hatch when she's on her side?" she finally asked. Her question was a good sign that she was calming down.

"She'll be all right," I replied.

"Is everything inside secure?"

"Everything is strapped down."

We stood there for a while and studied *Yankee Girl*. Her broad beam, combined with her heavy load of ballast, gave her enormous righting power. But how much exactly? When I'd managed to pull her down the first time, I had estimated the lift at her mast top to be about 100 pounds.

I glanced over at Sally. She weighed about 110 pounds, and probably a bit more dripping wet—which she was at the moment.

"Okay," I said, "let's get started. You hold her off while I pull her down."

Like a veteran sailor, Sally shoved *Yankee Girl* away from the dock with her foot. I jumped up and clutched at the shroud, put my weight on the wire, and swung out again. Once more *Yankee Girl* fought back on her way down.

"See if you can hold her!" I cried.

Nodding, Sally grabbed the mast and hooked her fingers over the tip.

"Have you got her?" I asked.

"Either I've got her or she's got me," she answered. "We'll know soon enough."

"Tell me if you think you can't hold her," I said, easing away. "I'll come back and help." I had visions of Sally being hoisted aloft and dangling from the mast; that would be all either of us needed.

"Boy, does she float high," Sally said, now lying nearly horizontal on the dock as she hung on to the mast.

Yankee Girl was far over on her side, her mast parallel to the water. In spite of the load she was carrying, no water entered her open hatch.

"Bring her down more if you can, Sal," I instructed.

I could see that *Yankee Girl* had at least six inches of free-board left before water could start leaking in. At an angle of more than 90 degrees, she still floated dry.

"Isn't this little girl fantastic?" I asked proudly. I turned to grin at Sally.

"Unbelievable," she agreed, shaking her head.

A quick inspection of *Yankee Girl*'s bottom showed that she had come through the storm unscathed. Working together, Sally and I eased up on her mast and let her go upright. The boat gained strength as she righted herself. When I could no longer hang on, I jumped on board.

"Let's put her away for the night," Sally suggested, "and go home."

"Fine with me," I replied. As Sally climbed on board, she shoved us off from the dock. We slipped silently into the freshly washed night.

The lights on the fringes of the shore twinkled on the smooth surface of White Bear Lake. The gloom and chill had lifted. The calm after this particular storm seemed more beautiful than any I had ever experienced.

It took only moments for the two of us to secure *Yankee Girl* to her mooring, double-lashing her to the buoy with a nylon rope and chain.

Afterward we rowed back toward the shore, watching *Yankee Girl*'s silhouette recede into the night. I was pleased with her. She had taken tonight's storm gallantly, and I was convinced that she was now ready for deeper waters—and for her true destiny.

Above us the stars came out, one by one.

"I really *was* worried about you," Sally said softly.

"I'm sorry about that," I answered. "But you know, Sal, that I don't take chances."

Yankee Girl had disappeared from sight. The lake was filling with stars. In between pulls on the oar, I repeated to myself:

I don't take chances.

II

The Birth of
Yankee Girl

"A man's reach should
exceed his grasp."
Robert Browning

By 9:30 A.M. on that hot July day
in 1977, I already had the double garage doors open. I had
been working for several hours, and my face and hair were
covered with the patina of sawdust that goes hand-in-hand
with building wooden boats.

Nine-year-old Vinette was the first of the neighborhood
children to show up. "What are you building now?" she
asked, barely controlling her mirth. "An airplane?"

This was all part of a ritual I was used to: me, the backyard
boatbuilder, versus the neighborhood kids. The kids usually
won.

"It's going to be a boat!" I laughed back, wiping my dusty
forehead with my shirtsleeve. Vinette had visited my "boat-

yard"—the garage attached to my house—many times before.

She inched closer; I could tell that she was interested in my latest project. Even in these early stages my little boat had ribs and a frame. It rested, upside-down, on one of Sally's kitchen chairs. And it *did* look capable of sprouting wings at any second.

"It could be a boat, I guess," Vinette acknowledged. "Going to take a trip in this one?"

"You never know," I answered. "Maybe someday. But for now I'm building it just to try out some ideas. It's kind of an experiment." I winked at her.

She winked back, then turned and slipped away. She would return, I knew, throughout the day, along with the rest of the neighborhood kids. Build a boat in your garage, I reflected, and you were bound to attract kids like kittens to milk.

I was glad Vinette hadn't asked me any more questions, however, for I had few answers. In fact, I myself was still full of questions about my latest attempt at boat-building. I had been hard at work for over a month now, and already I was facing more problems than I had bargained for.

The stringers—the fore and aft lengths of wood to which the planking would be attached—kept breaking, and I had not yet reached the most radical bends.

Time was running short. My summer break from the University of Minnesota would end in only a few weeks, and I'd have to begin preparing for my student teaching at Mariner High School in White Bear Lake—no matter what stage my boat was in.

Then there were the stomach cramps that refused to go away. I tried to ignore them, tried to block the pain from my mind. Sometimes I was successful, but not today. On this July morning the cramps seemed worse than ever.

I sat down for a moment with my arms folded tightly across my stomach. Maybe if I concentrated on something else I could forget about the pain. As usual, I turned my thoughts toward the boat.

Its design was new, unproven, and entirely my own. I had

always wanted to build such a boat, but lately I had begun to doubt whether *anyone* could build it, much less myself. After six months of planning and one month of construction, it seemed to be going nowhere. I closed my eyes and sighed.

I remembered the moment when the idea for the boat had first come to me. It had been about 2:30 A.M. in the middle of a bitterly cold Minnesota night. I had awakened with a start and stolen silently out of bed. Sally hadn't even stirred; after fifteen years of marriage, she was used to my getting up at odd hours, puttering around, and then crawling back under the covers.

After a quick detour into the kitchen for a snack, I had padded down the hall to my study and turned on the light.

The wind was rattling the frozen tree branches outside my window as I began sorting through the piles of papers on my drawing board. At first glance they seemed like a random and unfocused hodgepodge of notes, thoughts, and sketches. There were drawings I had made while waiting in doctors' offices; pieces of notebook paper I had scribbled on during university lectures; scraps on which I had written sudden inspirations or ideas while traveling.

Sally was right: I *was* a packrat. I saved everything!

Despite the rather disorderly appearance of my collection, though—a collection I had been working on for several years—it made sense to me. For every sketch, paragraph, and line was a variation on a single theme: boat building.

Just looking through my papers brought back a flood of memories. I had, after all, been fascinated by boats for over seventeen years. I had sailed them, built them, and even designed a few. I loved what they could do and what I could do with them. To me, sailing was the closest a person could come to complete freedom.

I smiled as I recalled my earliest sailing experiences. There had been plenty of capsizings, groundings, and near-collisions in those days. During the early 1960s, while I was in the Air Force, I took every opportunity to sail whenever and wherever I could. All I wanted was something that would float and somewhere to float it. I ended up in a number of pretty strange places—from reservoirs in Colorado and Kansas to minuscule prairie lakes in Nebraska.

The first boat I built by myself came out of a kit. A 15½-foot Snipe, she was a delight to sail and, with her varnished mahogany decks, a real beauty.

The first boat I designed was a 17-foot ocean-going miniature cruiser I christened *Yankee Doodle*. Some of the happiest months of my life were spent with her. In 1969-70, she made it possible for me to live out one of my biggest fantasies: sailing down the Mississippi River from St. Paul to New Orleans, then through the Caribbean and on to Panama.

By the time I arrived at the Canal I was so lonely for Sally that I called her and asked her to join me. Together we sailed from Panama to Ecuador. During that voyage I discovered what a great ocean sailor Sally is.

That was very nearly the last major trip I ever made, though. One day while Sally and I were cruising off the coast of South America, we noticed a pod of whales playing about a mile in the distance. Suddenly one 80-foot giant broke away from the group and charged our little boat. He came and came, the waves crashing over his blunt head. When he was only about 100 feet away, he stopped and watched us for a few minutes. Then he dove.

Sally and I held our breaths and prayed that he wouldn't decide to surface beneath us. If that happened, it would be all over. Moments later the whale erupted out of the sea in front of us and rose straight into the air. When he fell back into the water, the noise and the turbulence were devastating.

The whales stayed with us until nightfall, pounding the ocean with their huge, flat tails.

We got the message. As soon as we could, we put into Ecuador and sold *Yankee Doodle*. When we finally arrived back in Minnesota, I was so relieved to be home safe and sound that I vowed never again to attempt such an undertaking.

I should have known better. A few years later I was at it again, this time in a 15-foot trimaran of my own design named *Yankee Spirit*. In November, 1974, I set sail out of Miami, intending to make the Bahamas the first stop on a two-year solo voyage around the world. Within 53 hours I was back in Miami—exhausted, hallucinating, and close to a complete collapse.

I had discovered the hard way that we humans aren't as strong as we think we are. The sea had taught me a stern lesson, and I was forced to admit that I was neither physically nor psychologically disciplined enough to meet its challenge head on. The next day I sold *Yankee Spirit* and returned to Minnesota.

As the years went by, I often thought about my two "failures." I slowly came to realize that my attitude had had a great deal to do with what had happened each time. Twice I had set out to "conquer" the oceans—and twice I had been the one who was conquered. I began to understand that the only sensible way to cross any sea was by cooperating with it.

And that was what I fully intended to do during my next voyage. For there would, of course, be a next voyage. Only this time I would build a special kind of boat—one I would design myself, using everything I had learned from my previous experiences. It would be radically different from any boat that had ever been built before.

Spread out before me now were three years' worth of notes and sketches, questions and—I hoped—answers. As I looked over my assembled data, I began battling the contradictions that inevitably arose whenever I worked on my newest project. It seemed as if I had set impossible goals for myself, and in many ways I had. Yet I was determined to at least try to reach them.

What I had in mind was this: I wanted to build the smallest practical-sized sailboat capable of surviving a journey across the treacherous North Atlantic. At the same time it would have to be large enough to carry sufficient supplies for months at sea. And, even when loaded down with half a ton of provisions, it would still have to be unsinkable.

There was more to my plan. Though its sail area would be limited, the boat would nevertheless have to have a relatively good turn of speed. It would have to be very maneuverable. And, finally, it would have to protect its pilot—me—from the raging elements in some degree of comfort.

I scratched my head, reached for a clean sheet of graph paper, and wrote the date across the top: *January 16, 1977.* Then I marked off 40 squares. On the scale I was accustomed to using, four squares represented one foot. Somehow I knew that my boat would be no more than ten feet long.

Next I had to decide on the width of the beam. Here I knew I'd have to make some tradeoffs. Given the boat's length, the beam would have to be as wide as possible in order to provide both buoyancy and stability. If I made it too wide, though, the little boat would have to push its blunt bow through the water, and this would slow us down. But if I followed the conventional rule of thumb and made the beam one-third as wide as the boat was long, I'd end up with a craft only 3 feet 4 inches across. That would give me a faster boat, but not a very stable one, and it would never be able to carry the enormous load of supplies I'd need.

I decided to gamble. Bending over my sheet of graph paper once again, I marked off the equivalent of 5 feet 6 inches and penciled in the curve.

For a moment, I sat and stared at my handiwork. What I had just drawn didn't look like any boat I had ever seen. Instead, it looked like a sawed-off pumpkin seed. I shook my head in amazement.

At least I had taken the initial steps—that was something. For the first time in months, I felt an enormous sense of relief. I was on my way; I had made two major decisions. The ten-foot length was, I felt, as small as I could reasonably go and still end up with a boat capable of navigating the high seas.

And the five-and-a-half-foot beam would give me sufficient room and stability.

I was a little surprised at what I had come up with, because my ultimate goal had not been to design a boat that would be smaller than anyone else's. All I cared about was building a compact, manageable vessel that could carry me across the ocean. Despite its size, it would have to be a *real* boat that would handle like any other sailboat. It would have to tack into the wind, foot along well on a reach, and carry a normal complement of sails. It would, I hoped, be a craft that I could sail out on its own and aim for any port I steered for around the world.

I was most emphatically not aiming for a "drifter"—a boat that would have to be towed out to sea and left there to drift aimlessly with the ocean currents, only to be towed back in again. I wanted a boat whose priorities would be safety and reliability. A work boat—not a beauty queen—that could take me anywhere I desired.

I looked down once more at the outline of my chunky little craft. Then, satisfied, I turned off my study light and went back to bed.

When I awoke in the morning after only a few hours' sleep, I felt refreshed and invigorated. I knew that in the middle of the night I had turned my life around.

As usual, Sally was up before me and already sipping her first cup of coffee at the kitchen table. I sat down across from her and, without preliminaries, made my announcement: "I've decided to go ahead with my plan."

I watched her face closely as I waited for her response. I could tell that my news hadn't surprised her. She took another swallow of coffee, set her cup carefully on its saucer, and said, "There goes the garage for the next six months."

I was delighted. "I'll be out of there long before winter," I promised. "You'll have the 'boatyard' back before the snow flies."

That startled her. "When are you planning to sail?" she asked.

"I'll build the boat this summer, test it in the fall, and sail the Atlantic next summer."

"I think I'll have that second cup of coffee now," Sally said.

Little did I know how much planning, building, and testing were still to come. Putting those first few lines down on paper had been only the beginning. For the next three months, I spent every spare moment completing my design. That meant that after attending classes at the University every day to finish my education degree, I came home every night and hunched over my drawing board.

I sent off countless letters requesting information I'd need for my journey: navigation tables, pilot charts, sailing directions, Gulf Stream surveys, coast pilots, and navigational charts. I amassed data on wave heights, wind directions and strength, periods of calm, atmospheric pressure, precipitation, fog, traffic, currents, and even icebergs. I haunted the libraries of Minneapolis, St. Paul, and the suburbs, seeking out accounts of the singlehanders who had braved the North Atlantic before me. Although none had attempted the crossing in a boat as small as the one I envisioned, their experiences and insights would, I knew, prove invaluable. I devoured every word I could find.

Everything seemed to be going according to plan. Then, late one night, as I was leaning over my drawing board, I realized something that nearly put me into a panic. My boat would weigh about 700 pounds—but it would have to carry more than 1,000 pounds of supplies. And I hadn't even considered my own 155 pounds!

I stared at my figures in disbelief. Could a ten-foot boat really bear such a load? Or would it sit so low in the water that its deck would be awash—and it would be in constant danger of swamping?

I knew that I wanted to be able to take a motor. I'd need one in order to maneuver in port and stay out of the way of ships; the danger of being run down at sea was very real. A motor would also help during periods of calm when there would be no wind to push me along.

But that, of course, would add a lot of extra weight. And it would also mean that I'd have to carry gasoline. How much? As much as possible—maybe 50 gallons. Another 300 pounds.

"Gerry, old buddy," I said to myself, "you're setting impossible standards for yourself. Maybe you'd be better off sticking to teaching."

Another uncomfortable thought crossed my mind. If, in the middle of the ocean, I discovered that I had been wrong about something—anything—I would never have the chance to try again.

There was simply no room for mistakes.

I *had* set impossible standards for myself. The more I thought about them, the less sleep I got.

What I was attempting to do was to design a radically different type of boat, one which, unlike other sailboats, would carry no significant amount of ballast. Ballast is what pulls a sailboat upright again if a high wave or strong wind pushes it over on its side. But it can also drag a damaged boat to the bottom. I wanted my boat to float no matter what happened to it.

In addition, my boat would have to be a complete life-support system for at least 60 days. To be on the safe side, I'd have to plan for a 50 percent margin in case of accident or error. In other words, I'd have to carry with me everything I could possibly need for a 90-day voyage—all the way from a first-aid kit to a portable head. I'd have to have a compact galley and a means of washing dishes. And I'd need a radio so I could maintain contact with passing ships.

I'd also have to bring sufficient clothing to meet the changing conditions at sea. I'd need sweaters for the chilly nights, special foul-weather gear, and plenty of shirts and pants. Everything I'd read told me that I wouldn't be able to do my laundry on board; I'd have a hard enough time keeping myself clean. So I'd simply have to carry enough clothes to allow me to wear each item once and then throw it away.

Where, on my tiny boat, would I find room for all of my supplies?

By the middle of May, my stomach was beginning to hurt. This was a warning sign that not all was well. I had a history of ulcers, and I knew that I had to slow down. But how could I? I had only one short summer in which to carry out my plans—and my dream.

I began the actual construction at the beginning of June. At first everything went smoothly. My design called for the use of plywood as much as possible. The keel would be made of laminated plywood, the frame would be plywood, and so would the outer skin.

I had to keep my costs down. A few of my money worries were solved one day when the neighborhood kids told me about a hardware store that was going out of business. We all piled into my old station wagon and rushed to the store. There we found plywood sheets in various sizes that had been used as shelves and partitions. Some of them were painted green, but that didn't matter to me. I got the whole lot, along with some used two-by-fours, for a total of $20—a real bargain.

By the time we were ready to head for home, the station wagon was crammed full of kids and plywood and practically bottoming out on every pothole. I couldn't even back it up the driveway to the garage. So, working together, the kids and I unloaded part of the wood and carried it up to the house by hand. Some of the lumber was still full of nails, and a few young entrepreneurs made $2 pulling them out.

The first step in the construction of my boat involved laminating the keel, stem, and transom knee. In most boats these "backbone" elements are made up of many different sections of wood, each laboriously shaped and fitted into place. But I wanted to make mine in one piece using heavy plywood.

I began by gluing and screwing two sheets together. Then I added two more ¾-inch-thick plywood pieces to either side. When I finally finished the keel structure, it was 4½ inches thick.

So far my calculations were holding up. My little boat would have an enormously strong "back." And I had done it all in 20 hours of work.

I wondered whether the frame construction would go as easily. According to my design, the boat would have only four frames. But these would be radically different from conventional frames. To begin with, I would cut each of them from a single sheet of plywood, incorporating the deck crossbeams, the starboard bunk support, and the port storage area. This approach would give my little boat great strength. It yielded another dividend as well: when I laid out the patterns on ¾-inch plywood, I was able to zip out the parts in just a few minutes with my electric sabre saw.

As I worked on the frames, I started worrying again about the boat's size. It was going to be awfully small. I was especially concerned about the storage areas. If I couldn't take along enough provisions to sustain myself for at least 90 days at sea, I couldn't go. That was a problem I would eventually have to face.

I wondered, too, whether I'd be able to fit myself into the boat when it was finished. I decided to find the answer to that question now. After cutting the fourth frame, I laid it out on the floor and tried to curl myself along the top of it, approximating the sitting position I'd take inside the boat.

That was the moment when Sally chose to come looking for me.

"What's going on?" she asked.

"Something's definitely wrong," I answered. I kept trying to squeeze my body into the frame's contours. But no matter how much I turned and twisted, some part of me still hung out over the edge.

I was perplexed. I had designed the boat to my dimensions,

being especially careful to calculate my sitting height, my leg length, and even my shoulder width. But I simply wasn't fitting.

I lay there for a moment more with my feet in the air, feeling foolish. Then I sat up and announced, "Well, I guess I'll just keep on building and hope I'll fit when I'm done."

"Look at it this way," Sally joked. "You'll have the best example of 'sitting headroom' ever seen."

I could laugh, for I knew what she meant. I might fit inside the boat later—if I leaned backward and sort of scrunched myself in. I wondered, though, whether I could spend days or even months at sea in such an uncomfortable position.

Over the next few weeks, the pain in my stomach intensified. It seemed to get worse whenever I bent down—something I had to do frequently while building my boat. Finally I made an appointment to see my doctor. At the time I thought I might have a hernia. This pain was different from any I'd ever experienced.

As it turned out, I didn't have a hernia. I had an iliacic ulcer.

"We'd better operate and find out exactly what's happening," my doctor advised. A surgeon seconded his opinion. There was a chance that my ulcer might be malignant.

I was horrified. To have surgery at this stage would mean the end of my dream.

"If it's only an ulcer," I suggested, "then let's try to cure it some other way."

"It's up to you," my doctor answered, "but you're taking quite a chance."

I began following a diet that had helped me in the past: fresh foods, vitamin supplements, and frequent meals. I drank gallons of milk, consumed dozens of eggs, and ate six meals a day. Weakened by the pain in my stomach, I forced myself to keep moving and continued to make progress on my boat. Sometimes I felt so terrible that I could only put in four hours of work at a time, and a poor four hours at that.

I had reached the step in the boat's construction when I was laying the "stringers," the long, thin pieces of wood that run the length of the boat along its frame. To these I would eventually fasten the ⅜-inch plywood planking.

But the stringers refused to bend to the extreme curve of the bow. They kept breaking whenever I tried to pull them down. Once I succeeded in fitting two stringers to the bow, gluing them, and screwing them in place. Thinking I had the problem solved, I was walking wearily toward the doorway when, with a loud cracking noise, they broke. The pain in my stomach returned.

For a while I considered cutting the stringers further into the frame to lessen the curve. But I knew that this would only weaken the frames and reduce the displacement, causing the boat to float too low in the water.

Then I thought of reducing the thickness of the stringers. They were a vital part of the boat, though, and I couldn't afford to sacrifice any of the hull's strength. There was always the possibility that they would split when the first really big wave slammed into the hull.

I started having recurring nightmares—of enormous waves rolling over my boat, of the hull cracking in two, of me being washed overboard. Not only was I having trouble working during the day, I was also finding it hard to sleep at night.

One evening late in June, after cleaning up the garage, I sat down on an old chair beside the little wooden frame. Then I rested my head in my hands and just stared at the boat. I looked at the frames, the keel, and the few stringers that had not yet cracked. I examined every inch of the bow, trying to imagine a way of making the wood fit around it. All I could think of was: *it can't be done.*

By about 1 A.M. a sick feeling had come over me. After five months of planning and nearly a month of building, I seemed to have reached an impasse.

The boat would never work.

I would have to burn everything I'd done and start over again.

Filled with a deep sadness, I left the garage and dragged

myself to bed. Once there, I couldn't fall asleep. I tossed and turned as visions of the boat I wanted to build flashed through my mind.

I crawled out of bed and went to my drawing board. After marking off squares on a clean sheet of graph paper, I began drawing a new set of lines. When I finished, I studied my work in amazement. I had drawn the same little boat.

Frustrated, depressed, and thoroughly exhausted, I went back to bed. Sally rolled over and looked at me questioningly.

"It just isn't going to work, Sal," I said. "I think I'll have to burn her."

"Get some sleep," she recommended, "and don't worry. It'll look different in the morning."

I sighed deeply. The pain in my stomach clenched like a fist. I spent the rest of the night dozing fitfully.

By the Fourth of July weekend my ulcer was unbearable. Sally and I had driven up to the north woods, near Big Floyd Lake, to spend the holiday with my parents. I had hoped that the fresh air and change of scenery would help, but I was wrong. I was so ill that I stayed inside the cabin while Sally and my parents went fishing.

I wondered whether I would ever again be well enough to undertake *any* voyage. What if my ulcer flared up while I was alone at sea? How would I survive an attack in the middle of the ocean?

One evening Sally and I took a walk through the pines along the lakeshore.

"You've had ulcers before," Sally remarked, "and you've always gotten over them."

"When I get this sick, I lose my strength," I answered. "If the ulcer doesn't go away, I'll just have to give up."

"The first thing you need to do is to get your construction problems squared away," she said.

"I know, but I can't," I admitted. "And I'm running out of time. In six weeks I'll have to start getting ready for my student teaching."

She stopped and turned to face me.

"Listen to me, Ger," she said, and her voice was firm. "It's mostly a matter of psychological outlook."

I thought about her words in silence for a few moments. What she had said rang true. Everything that was happening to me was a direct result of what *I was doing to myself.* No one else was responsible for my unresolved fears, my impossible schedule, my inner conflicts. I would either have to solve my problems and straighten myself out inside—or forget about my dream.

Sally took my arm as we began walking back to the cabin.

"You've reached your low point," she said gently. "You're on your way up now."

She was right again. As had happened so many times in the past, her help and insight filled me with hope and courage.

I took a deep breath of the pine-scented air.

I could do anything I wanted to do.

Dawn broke at 4:30 A.M. on our first morning back in White Bear. I pulled on my old work clothes and went out to the garage to study my little boat's unfinished form once more.

It lay where I had left it in the middle of the garage, its frame covered with a fine layer of sawdust. The wood smelled wonderful to me.

Somehow I knew that I would solve the problem of the stringers today. Almost overnight, my attitude had changed. I had broken enough stringers; it was time to get serious.

I picked up a very thin, light piece of molding that I had been using to check the curves of the hull and laid it over the frame. Then, following a sudden inspiration, I moved it up to the treacherous curve at the bow.

It bent like a willow as I pressed it into place.

I stood there amazed. The solution had been at hand all

along; I had simply not allowed myself to see it. My mind had been too closed, too preoccupied.

Moving fast now, I put one end of the molding in a clamp against the transom and bent it forward around the hull all the way to the bow. It clung to the curve like a strand of spaghetti.

I took one of the 1¼-inch thick stringers and rushed over to my table saw. Then I ran it lengthwise through the saw and cut two narrow, pliable pieces. Racing back to the boat, I clamped the stringers to the frames, one on top of the other. The split pieces fit together easily around the curve.

I squeezed glue between the two pieces and laminated them together. Now they were the same thickness as before. The resulting stringer was the same size as the ones that had kept breaking on me. Since it was made up of two halves, though, it was far stronger.

I slumped down against the wall, relieved.

The thought that I had nearly given up—that I had nearly burned my little boat when I had been so close to victory— made me shiver. But this time the fear passed quickly. I had work to do.

The remaining stringers went on without a hitch. From this point on, I started to feel much better. And my stomach began to heal.

I thought back to what Sally had said only days earlier. She had been right—it *had* all been a matter of psychological outlook.

The next challenge facing me was the task of bending the ⅜-inch construction-grade plywood onto the frame. The thick wood had to fit exactly over the stringers and follow their curvature. Soon I began experiencing the same problems with the ply as I'd had with the stringers. Bending it was like flexing a steel spring; on the compound curve near the bow, it tended to break along the forward tapered edges.

In the past a setback like this would have caused me to fret and worry. But now I became thoughtful and determined. I knew I would find an answer—it was simply a matter of time.

The solution came to me almost immediately. I put a tea-kettle of water on the stove to boil. When I heard its whistle a few moments later, I took the troublesome ply out onto the driveway, went to get the kettle, and poured the boiling water directly over the wood.

When I hauled the ply back to the boat frame, I found that while the boiling water had made it more flexible, it was still not bending down the way it had to. I placed rags on top of the ply, heated more water, and saturated the rags. As I slipped and sloshed about, the boiling water did its job. When I finally tightened the clamps, the wood bent willingly.

It was clear that I would be able to build the hull I wanted. Nothing could stop me. Day by day, my stomach got better, and in three weeks the pain was gone.

Work on the boat now went quickly and joyfully. After gluing the ply and screwing it to the frames and stringers, I sanded the hull down with my auto body grinder, filled the screw holes with putty, and covered everything with overlapping layers of fiberglass. The keel area got four extra layers for added strength. When the "glass" was finally on the hull, I pulled my little boat out into the driveway to cure in the hot July sun. The whole structure weighed about 400 pounds. I propped the bow up on a kitchen chair so the air could circulate around it.

Singly and in pairs, the neighbors strolled over to inspect my latest project.

"It's an awfully small boat," one commented after studying its upside-down form for several minutes. "Going to do anything with it?"

"Nothing in particular," I answered. "I just want to see if it's possible to build a boat this small that'll sail well."

The kids came too, of course. When another neighbor asked, "How can you stand to have those kids around all day?" I responded immediately, "They make my day."

It was true. I looked forward to their visits. Each neighborhood kid was a character, and each was a great joy to me. They all loved to get involved.

"Can you find me a little piece of wood about this long?" I would ask Mike, holding up two fingers. He would rummage happily around the garage for just the right piece and come running back to me.

"Is this one okay, Ger?" he'd ask.

"Couldn't be better," I'd always answer.

Eight-year-old Kenny was a compulsive cleaner-upper. Freckle-faced, with auburn hair that stood out from his head like shocks of hay, he would come running over whenever the garage door went up.

"Hi, Ger," he'd say. "Whatcha doin'?"

"Got to work on my boat," I'd reply.

And then he'd ask, with a catch in his throat, "Can I help?"

I'd look at him critically. "Think you're old enough?"

"Sure," he'd say, puffing out his chest.

I'd nod. "First thing we'd better do is clean up. It's not safe to have a lot of stuff lying around underfoot." I'd pretend to look around, and Kenny's eyes would follow mine. I could predict what would happen next: Kenny would claim the biggest broom he could find and sweep out the entire garage.

When Kenny's parents learned what he was doing, they were amazed. "*Our* Kenny?" they asked. As it turned out, though, this was only the beginning for Kenny. On days when I didn't have anything for him to do, it wasn't unusual to see him out in front of his parents' house sweeping the street.

By the end of July I had seen so much of the neighborhood kids that I was able to identify adults by their resemblance to their offspring.

In time the kids started imitating me. They wanted to build their own boats.

"Better make a model first so you'll know how it's going to turn out," I'd advise. Then they'd "borrow" pieces of wood from the small box I'd set aside for them and, days later, proudly show me their creations: some lopsided, some with masts drooping to one side.

"*Very* interesting," I'd say, encouraging them.

When the day came to start painting the hull, the kids begged me to let them help.

"I don't have enough brushes," I said lamely.

"We'll get some from our dads," they chorused, and off they ran. Minutes later they were back, brushes in hand. I winced. Knowing what a beating the brushes would take, their fathers had given them the worst ones they had.

"Well," I said, thinking fast, "let's start with the inside first." This was something the kids could do even with beat-up brushes. Soon they went to work sloshing white paint around the bilges. They were in their glory; it was good fun for everyone.

When they tired of the job, I solemnly thanked them and suggested that they leave their brushes with me. They happily ran off to play, and I climbed back into the paint-spattered bilge to finish up.

Later I attacked the pile of brushes the kids had left behind. Needless to say, they were full of paint and their bristles were stiff as boards. I ended up working on them until 11 P.M. that night. Some of them were in better shape when they went back to their owners than they'd been in when the kids brought them over. I wished I could have seen some of the fathers' faces.

My own father, Louis, was not aware of my plans until one day late in the summer when he came by for a visit. I had even kept my secret during the Fourth of July weekend we'd shared up north. I hadn't yet thought of a suitable way to break the news to my parents—especially my mother, Jeanette. What could I say? "Guess what—I'm going to sail the North Atlantic in a ten-foot homemade boat"?

Dad arrived unexpectedly while I was in the middle of working. I resisted the urge to say anything and let him walk around the boat on his own for a few minutes. I could already tell that he wasn't fooled—he knew my latest project wasn't meant for White Bear Lake. After all, I'd been talking about an ocean voyage for years.

"How long is it?" he finally asked, squatting down beside the boat.

"She's a ten-footer," I replied, trying to stay calm.

There was a long silence. I wondered what he was thinking. Would he try to discourage me? Or would he keep his true feelings to himself? And what—this was an important question—would he tell Mother?

At last he straightened up and looked squarely at me.

"She's going to be strong, isn't she?" he said.

"She'll have to be," I answered, smiling. At that moment I knew that he understood exactly what I had planned.

Dad kept our secret, but it was inevitable that Mother would learn the truth sooner or later. On her birthday, my parents came over to our house for dinner. The moment they arrived, Mother decided that she wanted to see how our garden was progressing. The route to our back yard was through the garage. Mother took two steps into the "boatyard" and stopped abruptly.

"That had better not be another boat," she said.

"I'm afraid it is," I admitted uneasily.

"What do you plan to do with this one?" she asked.

"I haven't decided yet," I answered, stretching the truth a bit. "I'm only trying out some ideas."

"Just be sure that you don't sail it anywhere but on White Bear Lake," she warned. "That boat is much too small to take on the ocean."

I knew that I hadn't heard the end of it yet. Sure enough, she came up with one motherly ploy after another over the next few weeks.

"You know," she suggested one day, "with your woodworking skills, you could build a really pretty boat." She smiled brightly. "Something for the lake."

When I let that idea pass, she tried a new strategy.

"Look at these lovely wooden clocks," she exclaimed, unfolding a full-color brochure. "You can build one for me. I'll even buy all the parts and materials."

In spite of her attempts to distract me, I was ready by September to launch my creation in White Bear Lake. On a beautiful fall afternoon, Dad, Sally, and I loaded the little boat, still unnamed, onto my homemade trailer and drove to a launching ramp near Tally's.

I had spent all that day student teaching, and I had barely been able to keep my mind on my classes. Had my calculations been correct? Would my boat float on its lines?

This was it—the culmination of years of work.

I stepped the mast on the cabin top and hung the rudder. Then, with Sally on one side of the boat and Dad on the other, I carefully backed the trailer into the lake.

As soon as the boat's transom touched the water, it began to float. But as more of the hull entered the lake, it suddenly lurched to one side.

Sally clutched at the shroud and screamed. "It's rolling over! It's rolling over! Stop! Stop!"

Dad grabbed the other side. Together he and Sally supported the boat, which was tilting wildly.

"Better get her back on the trailer," he said.

I tried to crank the boat ahead, but it was caught on the end roller and wouldn't move. Dad and Sally couldn't let go. My project was teetering on the edge of disaster.

Quickly I tightened the steel winch cable as far as it would go and then plunged into the cold water. Reaching under the transom, I shoved with all my strength.

With a groan, the boat nudged over the roller. I sloshed back to the winch and cranked hard. Though the boat was still angled crazily off to one side, it began to inch forward on the trailer. I jumped into the car and pulled the trailer up the ramp, where the three of us worked hastily to unstep the mast.

I was thoroughly embarrassed. I had expected my boat to float high without any weight inside. I was going to load it down with ballast later, once I knew what was needed. But I should have known better than to step the mast before launching; that additional weight up high had proved to be too much.

Grateful that there hadn't been any witnesses at the ramp, the three of us slunk home.

It had not been a very auspicious launching for a boat I intended to sail across the North Atlantic.

III

Preparing for the Voyage

"They can because
they think they can."
Virgil

Snow draped the small boat parked beside the driveway during the winter of 1977-78, and the neighbors forgot about it. But my work for the journey continued as I searched for solutions to what appeared to be insurmountable problems. Although my attitude remained positive, niggling doubts were beginning to creep in.

I was confident that my boat would be strong enough; that had never worried me. Despite the disastrous first launching, I knew that with proper preparations and sufficient ballast it would survive any voyage. The six layers of plywood on the stem made it a virtual battering ram—which it would have to be, since it would literally punch through a million waves in its lifetime. And the fiberglass sheathing around the ⅜-inch plywood gave it a hull like a walnut.

What I hadn't yet been able to determine was whether my ten-foot boat would hold enough provisions for a transatlantic crossing. It was virtually indestructible, but *I* wasn't. That boat would have to keep me alive. Would it be able to? Whenever I asked myself that question, I always came up with the same answer: I really didn't know. All I had to go by was theory.

From what I had learned from my research, I figured that the crossing would take about 60 days. That meant that I'd need to take at least two months' worth of food, water, clothing, and other supplies. But the 3,800 miles of the Atlantic I'd be facing were notoriously fickle. They could stop a boat dead for days at a time, drive it backwards, or even disable it. For safety's sake, I'd have to load up with sufficient provisions for a full three months at sea. If anything went wrong, it would be a long way to the next supermarket.

I began by calculating my food and water needs. Assuming that I'd be eating regularly, I'd have to plan for five or six cans of food per day. I could, for example, have a can of milk and some granola for breakfast, a large can of chili and a small can of corn for lunch, and some canned peaches and stew for dinner.

I began multiplying figures. Five cans of food per day times 90 days equaled—and here I gasped—*450 cans*. Cans typically come in cases of 24. In other words, I'd have to carry the equivalent of *19 cases* of cans in various sizes, some large and some small.

How on earth would I ever be able to fit 19 cases of cans inside a ten-foot hull?

I started considering alternatives. What about dehydrated foods? They wouldn't take up much space—but they were awfully expensive. And I'd have to bring along water to mix them with, so I wouldn't really be saving any significant amount of space. It looked as if I'd have to take cans after all.

Thinking about water made me wonder how much I'd need for drinking purposes. I began keeping track of my daily consumption by drinking out of a measuring cup. For the first several days I drank two gallons of water per day. That, multiplied by 90 days, equaled 180 gallons. There was no way I could squeeze that much water into my boat.

Then, with a sense of relief, I realized that I was craving more water than I needed simply because I was thinking about it all the time. After several days of concentrated effort, I got my consumption down to one gallon per day. This still meant that I'd have to carry 90 gallons—another impossible figure.

In about a week I had settled down to a more regular, less anxiety-prone consumption of ⅓ gallon per day. I supplemented that with other liquids, such as small cans of apple or grape juice or V-8. Thirty gallons of water was a more manageable quantity, but for insurance I'd have to bring along several little cans of juice, too. Thirty gallons of water, plus 450 cans of food, plus an unknown quantity of canned juice—all of that would have to fit inside one tiny hull.

Soon my mind was bombarded by more questions. What if salt water got into my supplies and ruined some of the canned goods? What if some of the water containers broke because of the violent motion of the high seas? And could my little boat safely bear such an enormous load—or would it sit so low in the water that we'd be in constant danger of swamping?

I got another shock when I totaled up the weights of the cans and containers I'd figured on so far. With its hull packed solid, my boat would displace over 2,000 pounds!

I'd built it to be unsinkable, but there were limits to what it could take. And what if it were holed and flooded or sprang a leak? Obviously I couldn't carry flotation tanks or even foam for flotation. There wouldn't be room.

I struggled with these problems for days. Then, all at once, I had an inspiration. It was so obvious that I wondered why no one had thought of it before. Perhaps the provisions *themselves* could serve as both ballast and flotation.

Late one afternoon, while I was in the middle of proving my theory, Sally walked into the bathroom and found me leaning over the tub. I had filled it with water. Cans of various sizes were spread out on the floor.

"What are you doing now?" she asked. "Drowning cans?"

"Look at this," I said, carefully placing a small can of Green Giant corn in the water. Then I sat back to watch.

"It floats!" I exclaimed triumphantly.

Sally stood there silently with her arms folded across her chest.

"Now look," I added with glee, dropping a can of baked beans into the tub. It plopped into the water and promptly sank.

"You never liked beans anyway," Sally said. I knew that she understood what I was doing.

My discovery opened the door to a possible solution. I still didn't know how I was going to take a total of 450 cans with me—but if I did, they would weigh only a little more than 50 pounds when submerged.

Next I did some taste testing. If I were going to be stuck in the middle of the ocean with a limited food supply, I'd better like what I brought along. I went to the store and bought single cans of everything I could even imagine eating—different brands of chili, stew, fruits, vegetables, and so on. Over the next few months I devoured them all, rating them on a scale ranging from "excellent" to "awful." Few foods made it into the "excellent" category, but there were enough of them to provide the backbone of my menu. Toward the end of my gustatory foray, I wondered whether I'd ever be able to look at another can of chili again.

I also began making beef jerky. An excellent source of protein, it keeps forever. I had tried many commercial products but liked none of them; some were too smoky, and some contained too much garlic or onion.

After I finally came up with my own recipe, I started

haunting the neighborhood butcher. I quickly became a familiar face around his shop. I was the only person he knew who would order several pounds of sirloin tip and then ask to have every ounce of it sliced paper-thin.

At first he was puzzled by my request. "What are these supposed to be?" he wanted to know. "See-through steaks?"

"I found a great recipe in a magazine," I joked. "It tells you how to have steak every night for only four dollars a month."

My recipe involved marinating the beef in a special concoction of seasonings and then drying it very slowly. I tried using the oven, but that dried out the beef too quickly. After a period of trial and error, I settled on the ideal jerky-making technique. I spread the meat out on the oven racks and, instead of turning the oven on, plugged in Sally's hairdryer and set it inside. The steady stream of gentle heat worked perfectly.

During the first few days the kitchen was filled with a pleasant aroma. After weeks of full production, though, the odor had taken over the whole house. One day Sally couldn't stand it any longer.

"This place smells like a dead buffalo," she complained.

"Be patient," I begged. "I only have a few more batches to go."

My supply of beef jerky, when combined with the canned goods I planned to take, would provide me with plenty of food. But storing water was turning out to be more of a problem than I'd expected. In some containers it picked up a bad plastic taste; in others mysterious green things began to grow, one of which reached the size of an egg yolk before I finally threw it out.

I collected different kinds of containers, filled them with water, and stored them on our basement steps for several months. Whenever I sampled them, I recorded my findings. Meanwhile both Sally and I worried about tripping over them on our way down the stairs.

I couldn't seem to come up with a solution. Those containers that didn't affect the taste of the water were either the wrong shape or not strong enough to survive the journey. Then one day, while I was topping off the car battery with distilled water, the answer came to me. I realized that although that water had been sitting in the garage for two years and had been opened many times, it still looked clean and clear. I poured some into a glass and was delighted to find that it tasted as good as it looked.

That settled it: I would carry 30 gallons of distilled water in their original plastic jugs. But I'd have to be careful to choose only those with screw tops and test them to make sure that they'd stay closed.

I would use plastic containers for other purposes as well. Many of my extra provisions and a lot of gear would go into wide-mouthed one-gallon jars that had originally held institutional mayonnaise, ketchup, and mustard. I could get an unlimited supply of these from Mariner High School, where I was student teaching; all I had to do was to let the cooks and a few of the custodians know my plans, and I soon had more than I needed.

I had been wondering where I would store my clothing. As it turned out, the plastic containers from the high school cafeteria would serve this function too. I learned that by rolling a shirt very tightly—with Sally holding the other end—I could reduce it to the size of a hot-dog bun. Seven rolled shirts fit neatly into one container.

In fact, my little "suitcases" could do double duty by keeping my clothing absolutely dry and serving as flotation. Even though a filled container weighed two or three pounds, it still had five or six pounds of buoyancy when it was placed in water. I decided to store everything I could in these plastic wonders, put them in sail bags, and lash them to various nooks and crannies inside the hull.

Each problem I solved seemed to lead straight into another. I knew now where I'd keep my clothes, but I also knew that I'd never be able to wash them and hang them up to dry on a ten-foot boat. In addition, clothing that gets wet with salt water can't be dried out. That meant that I'd only be able to wear things once before I'd have to throw them away. I'd need a fresh set of clothing for nearly every day of my trip.

I began making some calculations. I would have to take at least 40 shirts, 20 pairs of pants, 35 pairs of socks, six sweaters, and 35 sets of underwear—along with the plastic containers to put them in. All of this would somehow have to fit inside my little craft.

I started thinking about other things I might need along the way for protection from the elements. I'd have to make sure to take good care of myself at sea; I knew I'd tire quickly from the constant wetness, cold, and motion. I wasn't planning on having to tough it out, and I meant to take every possible precaution.

I prowled the local libraries at night, reading the accounts of other voyagers. Their books told me what I would need to beware of: dehydration, sunburn, dampness, bitter cold, windburn, abrasion, loneliness, isolation, hallucinations, and fatigue that could spread as far as the eye sockets. I might encounter storms that lasted for days on end and mountainous waves that would roar over my tiny boat.

The more I read, the more nervous I became. I redoubled my efforts to take every conceivable precaution. I was sure that my boat could survive the journey, but I wasn't convinced *I* could—or that it was possible to squeeze everything I'd need on board. And there was no way I'd find out until I actually set sail. I was on my own; no one before me had ever done what I was trying to do.

Every day I had more questions than answers. Of particular concern to me was my still unproven theory of stability and buoyancy. This theory was central to the success of my voyage—and again I had no way of knowing whether it would work.

In order to carry its sail area, my boat would need a certain amount of weight in the form of ballast. In most boats this is provided by lead or steel weights in the bilges or keel. But there are two disadvantages to this type of ballast: it takes up space, and it can pull a flooded boat to the bottom.

What I planned to do was to use my provisions as ballast. That way I wouldn't be wasting any space. And, if the boat were ever swamped, they would automatically double as flotation. I already knew that my 400 pounds of canned goods would weigh only about 50 pounds in the water. My 30 gallons of distilled water would weigh 240 pounds in the air but would float in salt water. Whatever gasoline I carried would provide two pounds of buoyancy per gallon when submerged, and the one-gallon containers filled with clothing and dried foods would be worth about five pounds of buoyancy each.

When combined with the fact that my boat was made of wood, all of this floatable "ballast" would make us virtually unsinkable. Yet the more than 1,000 pounds the boat would carry below the water line would give us tremendous stability.

The only things that would sink, in fact, were the tools, the radios, and the motor. In the event that we were flooded, I could throw the radios and the motor overboard.

If my ideas proved correct, in other words, I would have the safest boat in the world. *If.*

One day I discussed my theory with my friend Bill Mezzano.

"It sounds good," he said, "but what happens when your supplies are used up?"

"I think I'll be able to replace that weight with salt water," I answered. More theory.

All winter long I continued making lists of items I'd need to carry. By now I had filled several pages in my notebook. Whenever I stopped to think, I came up with something new. A radar reflector so my little boat wouldn't be run down by ships. Fire extinguishers, flare guns, smoke bombs, and sea anchors. Insect repellent. A hatchet in case I ever had to break out of the cabin. Waterproof putty for repairing holes in the hull if I had a collision. My "Gear to Buy" and "Still to Do" lists seemed to stretch on forever.

And every addition meant another expense. Though my costs during the summer for the basic hull and sails had totaled only $688, I had been adding gear steadily since then. I'd saved money by building the trailer myself, but I'd still had to buy the materials—the axle, wheels, and springs. I'd had to purchase a motor, one that was both rugged and easy on gas, and I'd managed to find a four-horsepower Evinrude on sale for $300—a real bargain. But then I'd had to buy an outboard bracket, a fuel tank, and extra hardware. I had an antenna, but no radio yet. A few more items here and there and I was already up to $1,637. The tab for a solo transatlantic crossing was turning out to be steeper than I'd bargained for.

About the only item that didn't cost me much was my clothing. For years Sally had been accusing me of saving everything and never throwing anything away, and now I was glad I had. I could simply pull out dozens of old shirts, shorts, and pants I'd collected—enough, I hoped, for my months at sea.

The winter went by quickly, and I looked forward to the spring and more sailing. Sally and I had managed to do some during the fall of 1977, and the results had been encouraging. In September, at the first launching, I had made the mistake of stepping the mast when there was no ballast in the boat. But I had learned my lesson. Before going out again, we loaded it with my old lifting weights, rocks from the lakeshore, and a few bags of sand. That at least brought it down to the sailing lines.

It wasn't much fun to scrape ice and snow off the boat every time we wanted to go sailing, but we did it anyway. Once, on an especially chilly afternoon, I dressed up in two pairs of pants, two coats, a scarf, a cap, and—as a final touch—a pair of tennis shoes to keep me from slipping. The shoes proved to be a bad choice. Once they got wet, I may as well have been barefoot.

During those frostbitten excursions onto the lake, Sally sometimes huddled below.

"If it gets any colder," she said one day, her teeth chattering, "we'll be able to put runners on this boat of yours and enter it in the ice races."

In October we had even tried a spinnaker test. Sally had gone forward and hoisted the billowy 180-square-foot sail when suddenly the wind hit us. The boat heeled wildly, and in seconds we were running out of control.

Ahead of us were two fishermen bundled up in heavy parkas and scarves. They caught sight of us as we bore down on them, and the look on their faces was something to see.

"Don't panic!" I yelled at Sally as I clambered to the bow. Gathering in the icy sail, I avoided the fishermen's eyes as we careened past their transom.

"Why do I always end up with the tiller when things get desperate?" Sally wanted to know.

That had been our last sail of the season. With numb fingers we took out the ballast, hauled the boat up onto the trailer, and brought it home. Then we stored it, uncovered, off to one side of the driveway with its bow tilted upward to allow for water runoff. To keep it from sinking into the ground during the spring thaw, we placed the trailer wheels on boards. And there it remained during the winter of 1977-78, frozen into a snowbank.

But my little boat had shown real potential. Even on those blustery fall days, it had done everything I'd asked. It had run downwind with great authority and an almost rock-like solidity; it had reached with good balance; and—wonder of wonders for a boat that size—it had even pointed up into the wind with steadiness and speed. Because it lacked a real centerboard, I had feared that it wouldn't be able to point well and that its windward performance would be less than adequate. But instead my boat had consistently behaved with competence and grace. It had, as I was beginning to learn, a distinct personality and even a streak of stubbornness.

At first I had planned to call it *Yankee Limey*, since I'd be sailing it from the United States to England. Somehow, though, that name didn't quite capture my feelings. For I was becoming enchanted with my creation.

"What a sweetheart you are," I'd say, patting her painted side. "What a sweet little girl."

And so I named her *Yankee Girl.*

I started working on the boat again during the late spring chill. Pressing Sally's hairdryer into service once more, I ran it inside *Yankee Girl* and heated up the cabin to a tolerable temperature. Then I repainted the bilges, built shelves, and strapped more equipment inside.

Meanwhile the mass of gear I'd already accumulated weighed heavily on my mind. I still didn't know where I was going to put it all.

Throughout the summer of 1978, I spent as much time as possible testing my boat on the water. For a while I tried living on it at night. Sally and I would watch the 10 P.M. news together and, when it was over, kiss each other good night. Then I'd grab my flashlight, a couple of eggs, some bread, and a sleeping bag and head out to *Yankee Girl*, now moored in front of Tally's. I'd take her out onto the lake, catch some sleep, and cook myself breakfast in the morning. I usually rejoined Sally before it was time for us both to leave for work.

I learned something new almost every day—or night. For example, I started out by sleeping under a blanket. But I soon discovered that I couldn't keep it on me as I rolled about, so I switched to a sleeping bag.

My first "bed" was a four-inch foam cushion extending roughly from the transom to near the bow along the starboard side of the boat. Although it allowed me to stretch out full length, the foam wasn't dense enough, Sally and I took out one inch of the foam and replaced it with a firm piece of leftover carpet pad—a great improvement.

I gradually grew accustomed to living in such a small space, and I began to love the hours I spent aboard *Yankee Girl.*

Night after night, she gently rocked me to sleep.

It wasn't long before my unusual behavior started attracting attention. One Saturday morning, after sleeping late, I shoved back the hatch, stood up, stretched, yawned—and only then noticed the family in the rowboat beside me. I blinked at them, and they stared back. None of us knew what to say.

As they rowed past, one of the kids turned to his parents and asked, "What's that guy doing? Sleeping in his boat?"

"Of course not," the father answered. "He couldn't sleep in there."

"Then what *was* he doing?" the boy wanted to know.

"Never mind," said his father. "Never mind."

I wondered for a moment what they had been thinking. Finally I decided to forget about it and just enjoy the beautiful day.

The sun was beaming down on me, and the lake was blue and clear. I bobbed about on my little boat, fixing breakfast according to a routine I'd established weeks earlier. I had found a miniature butane stove that fit neatly into a plastic dishpan, along with dishes and silverware. Pulling out my "galley," I hung the gimbaled stove on its mounting in the 18 x 24-inch footwell and lit the flame with a welder's sparking tool. Then I dropped two eggs into the pan, scrambled them with a fork, and in less than a minute they were done. After adding a dash of salt and pepper, I ate them right out of the pan, gazing at the idle row of boats tied to their moorings.

I was second from the end and nearly out of sight of Tally's dock, so few of the shoreline "regulars" could watch my comings and goings. I doubted that even Millie, Tally's watchful manager, knew that I was sleeping on my boat. For that I was glad. I was learning to live with most of the derisive comments leveled at my little girl, but it still hurt when someone asked, "Does that thing *really* sail?"

When I was done eating I washed my pan and fork in the lake. As I peered down into the water, dozens of tiny "fingerlings" suddenly came out of nowhere to snap up the bits of egg I rinsed from the pan.

Before long Larry, one of the dockboys, rowed out for a visit. Whenever he could sneak away from Millie, he usually made a beeline for my boat.

"Hi, Ger," he greeted me. "How's it going?"

"Fine," I replied. "How about something to eat?"

"Well, I guess so, if it isn't too much trouble. . . ."

Larry was always in the mood for a snack, and I carried plenty of food on board: beef jerky, fruit, crackers, and innumerable cans of juice.

With an apple in one hand and a can of juice in the other, he was ready to ask his favorite question.

"How was sailing last night?"

Larry loved to sit in his rowboat alongside *Yankee Girl*'s transom and listen as I described my most recent moonlight sailing experience. And I loved to talk about it. The ritual made us both happy.

I found it hard to understand why people did so much sailing during the day, in the glare of the hot sun, and so little at night. If they'd only wait until the stars came out—past the twilight hours, when the mosquitoes were ferocious—they'd find beautiful sailing. Night winds are steadier than day winds, and the moon provides plenty of soft, silvery light. In the absence of motorboats, fishermen, and water skiers, the lake is incredibly peaceful and serene.

I spent a lot of time staring up at the night sky as I sailed. I could see Polaris, the Big Dipper, and all of the stars that glitter in our northern skies. Sometimes it seemed as if I could reach up and touch them—or as if *Yankee Girl*'s mast could sweep them from the sky.

I knew that over the north Atlantic, thousands of miles away, the stars would look the same as they did over this small Minnesota lake. In a year, if all went well, I'd be there to see them. I had definitely decided to wait a full year before embarking on my voyage; I wanted to get as much experience with *Yankee Girl* ahead of time as I could.

I remembered some of the things I'd learned from my reading. The ancient Polynesians had used the stars to navigate between remote islands in the vast Pacific. Arab traders had used them to find their way as they crossed the desert in caravans; many stars, in fact, had Arabic names. The Arabs needed to be familiar with the stars for another reason as well: in order to pray toward Mecca, they had to know in which direction to turn. The stars always told them.

Out of my romantic night sailing came some practical improvements. I was soon able to handle the boat in the inkiest blackness. Realizing that red lights would help my night vision, I covered both the compass light and a flashlight with red plastic. I also kept a white flashlight on hand to signal other boats. I carried no running lights and had decided not to carry them at sea; my boat was so small that they would only confuse people who happened to notice them. Due to *Yankee Girl*'s size, I was required only to shine a flashlight on my sails to alert others of my presence.

During the nights aboard my little boat, I had ample time to think about my transatlantic adventure. Although looking up at that awesome sky made me feel very small, I could sense that my dedication to the journey was growing. What a thrill it would be to sail my tiny vessel across one of the world's greatest oceans!

I wondered what unfulfilled dreams other people kept hidden inside themselves. If only they'd realize that the first steps are the hardest, that even a dream only partially experienced is better than no dream at all. For years I'd believed that a person with the right combination of interest and perseverance could invariably do one of two things: either achieve his or her dream, or have a wonderful time trying. And sometimes the goal itself wasn't all that important—it was the learning and the sense of personal satisfaction along the way that mattered the most.

Maybe I was too involved in my project to read the signs that told me to hesitate, to turn back, to wait. Maybe I was blind to the realities of what I wanted to do. I had been studying and dreaming, planning and figuring for years, but there were still many questions I simply couldn't answer. I knew that *Yankee Girl* handled exceptionally well—better than I'd ever thought possible—but I hadn't yet been able to determine whether she'd carry the half ton of provisions I'd need.

At any rate, I was satisfied with the progress I'd made so far. No one could ever take that away from me.

I didn't spend all of my time on board *Yankee Girl* engaged in such serious thinking. Occasionally something happened on shore to distract me. One night, while I was gazing up at the stars and listening to the familiar slap of waves on the hull, I caught a whiff of what smelled distinctly like beef stew.

Gathered around a campfire on the western edge of White Bear Lake, members of the local VFW were brewing booya in 55-gallon drums.

I could see the figures silhouetted against the fire, but I knew that they couldn't see me.

"Come here and taste this stuff," I heard one of the cooks say. "Think it's picking up flavor from the drums?"

There was a pause and then a cough as another chef sampled the delicacy.

"Where did you get these drums?" the second man asked, nearly choking. "From your garage?"

"No, they're brand new," the first cook insisted.

"Pass me another beer," someone else said.

Feeling slightly mischievous, I decided that this was as good a time as any to test a new piece of equipment: my flare pistol.

I cocked it, aimed it into the air, and pulled the trigger. Nothing happened.

From across the water came the clank of beer cans being tossed into a pile.

I took out another flare. This one rose 60 feet into the air, ignited, and burned brightly as it descended.

The reaction from the shore was instantaneous.

"What the heck was that?" a voice asked.

"Did you see what I just saw?" said another.

"There was a red light over there," a third chimed in.

"You've had too much to drink," a fourth accused.

"No, by golly, I saw a red light over the lake."

I waited a decent interval and then let another flare go.

"There it is again!" shouted a voice excitedly. "I told you I saw it!"

"Call the rescue squad," said someone else. "There's something out there!"

By now they were all standing in front of the fire looking out into the darkness. None of them moved a muscle.

Finally one man stretched and sighed.

"Well, whatever was out there, it's gone now," he said.

"That reminds me," someone else began, "of the night we hit the beach at Anzio. . . ."

And they were off on another round of war stories.

By August I had logged many miles and hours aboard *Yankee Girl*. But I still hadn't come up with a way to convince my mother that my trip was a good idea.

As we'd done the year before, Sally and I invited my parents to dinner for Mother's birthday. True to form, Mother had plotted a new diversionary tactic.

"If you want to prove that you can live on a ten-foot boat for three months," she ventured hopefully, "why don't you just sail back and forth across White Bear Lake until Thanksgiving?"

"It just wouldn't be the same," I answered, doing my best to be serious. "Besides, I'm only going on a pleasure cruise. You'll probably want to sail the boat yourself when I get back."

"Hardly," she replied.

Although she managed to throw a few reproachful looks my way during dinner, the subject wasn't raised again.

Throughout that evening, as the four of us shared a good

meal and some pleasant conversation, I felt a sense of urgency creeping up on me like a shadow. I was 38 years old; by the time I set sail I'd be 39. In terms of what my body could stand, I didn't have many years left in which to realize my dream.

Later that night, as I sat alone in my study, I wondered if perhaps I shouldn't have taken some shortcuts. If I'd had someone else design a boat for me, I could have saved months. Or I could have designed it myself and had someone else build it. Or I could have just bought a boat and modified it.

I shook my head. Any of those approaches would have been wrong for me. I knew that I had done what I'd needed to do. The time, the energy, and the money required so far had all been mine. And the final satisfaction would be mine too.

That fall I faced yet another problem. Aggravated by long periods of boat building and sailing, my knee had been locking up. There were times when I couldn't straighten out my leg without help, and the pain was steadily growing worse. This was something I couldn't take care of on my own, so in October I had surgery. It proved completely successful, and the days I spent recuperating gave me a chance to catch up on my reading.

I wasn't the only one having problems, though. Over the months, our house had become an overgrown ship's store. Sally had suffered in silence for a while, but I could detect rumblings on the horizon.

One evening, while I was bending over a piece of equipment on the dining room floor, she tapped me on the shoulder.

"Ger, I can't walk through this place anymore without tripping over something," she said.

I looked around. Gear was strewn everywhere. There were radio antennas, charts, cameras, books, magazines, kites, plastic containers, clothing, and provisions. There were sea anchors, a tape recorder, jars of nails, packets of screws, ropes, cables, a paddle, a megaphone, two plastic sextants, three compasses, a massive first-aid kit, and butane cylinders for the stove. Every item was in some stage of being inspected, tested, unpacked, packed, or simply awaiting stowage.

Even the garage was full. I'd decided to let *Yankee Girl* spend the winter of 1978-79 indoors; the cars had been assigned to the snowdrifts in the driveway.

Sally was right. Things were getting out of hand.

"I'm never going to get it all in," I said glumly. "It'll never fit. I'm just going to have to squeeze in what I can and make some hard decisions about what to leave behind."

I turned to Sally and patted her arm.

"I promise to have everything out of here in a couple of months," I told her.

"I'll be glad when the mess is gone," she admitted. "But then you'll be gone, too. That's the part I won't be glad about."

"Just think of how nice it'll be," I laughed. "The house will be spotless again, and I'll be out of your hair."

"You can stay," she said, finally smiling. "But that stuff has got to go!"

I had to keep much of my gear in the house because it was simply too cold to store it anywhere else. The bitter Minnesota winter could ruin some of the more delicate pieces of equipment. I needed to decide soon where I would put everything, though, so at night I'd bundle up in several pairs of pants, my down jacket, and a muffler and head out to *Yankee Girl*. Occasionally I brought Sally's hairdryer inside the cabin for warmth.

I had questions not only about weight and bulk but also about distribution. I'd have to store heavy items low, since they'd be my "working"—and, in fact, only—ballast. Light things could be stashed higher.

Sometimes when I came up with an especially clever solution to a storage problem, I shared it with Sally.

"Hey, Sal," I said one night, coming into the kitchen and stamping my feet from the cold. "I found a great place to put the poncho."

She zipped up her coat, pulled on her boots, and followed me back out to the garage.

"Look at how well it fits here," I said, pointing. "And look at where I've got the sextants."

Both of my Davis sextants were tucked neatly into crisscrossing shock cords fastened to the ceiling of *Yankee Girl*'s cabin. There they would be both accessible and safe from the salt water that could ruin their mirrors. Since they were ultralight, I could afford to carry them high inside the boat. Even though they'd only cost about $20 apiece, they deserved to be taken good care of; along with my compass, they'd be the only navigational tools I'd have.

I was obsessed with details. I spent hours trying to decide where to store such a seemingly insignificant item as a pair of scissors. Like everything else in the boat, it would have to be easily reachable. But, because it was made of metal, it would have to be kept away from the compass or it would affect the magnetic heading. And it would have to be secured somehow so it wouldn't stab me in the back if it came loose during a storm.

Finally I decided to put the scissors inside a plastic tumbler along with my silverware. The tumbler wouldn't just be a storage place, of course; I'd use it to drink out of as well. It, in turn, would go inside the plastic dishpan that held my small butane stove and my single stainless-steel pot.

The stove took careful planning. I figured that I'd need at least 16 cans of butane fuel for my voyage, but for safety's sake I added an extra eight. I'd have to use extreme caution when storing them, since a rusty can leaking gas would have the potential to cause a disastrous explosion. I ended up stowing the butane near the transom.

It was unlikely that anything would go wrong with my stove, but I was determined that if I made any miscalculations they would be in the direction of safety. So I purchased ten cans of sterno for backup.

I chose many items for my trip in the hope that they'd do

double duty. My poncho, for example, was cut in such a way that it could be used to catch rain if my supply of drinking water ever ran out. I smiled whenever I saw it. A large square of floral-print oil cloth, it wasn't very nautical—but it would work.

Even my plastic water containers would serve two functions. As soon as I consumed their contents, I'd fill them with sea water for ballast.

Each day I looked over the long list of supplies I'd already accumulated. It included an unbelievable 118 batteries—C's, D's, double A's, and 12-volts for my various flashlights, strobe lights, radios, and the tape recorder. There were spare bulbs for the flashlights, a barnacle scraper, and a snorkel and mask to wear when I cleaned the bottom of the boat. I'd given in and added a set of running lights, but I wouldn't use them unless I had to.

Details and more details! Sometimes their sheer numbers exasperated me, but I knew that each was important. The smallest item, no matter how insignificant it might seem on land, could be crucial at sea. Every successful adventurer I'd read about had depended on planning and foresight far more than luck. And there was always the possibility that *Yankee Girl* and I would ultimately succeed—or fail—because of a single detail.

I had never put much stock in the idea of fate, and I wasn't about to treat this journey as a series of chance events, a time when I'd be cast adrift in a universe of incalculable dimensions. Instead, I surrounded myself with details—all of which could be isolated, analyzed, and acted upon. I meant to be in control at all times.

As the winter drew to a close, I looked back at the work I'd done over the past several months. I had thought everything through again and again. I had spent hours, sometimes 16 a day, going over every step of my plan—its function, its strengths, its weaknesses. I had made and discarded countless choices, insisting that the final one be the best it could be. My sense of personal commitment to my dream was very strong.

I was eager for spring. I'd use that time to tie up loose ends. For I'd made up my mind: I would set sail in June.

In March I decided to buy some additional life insurance. I wondered if, under the circumstances, I'd qualify for extra coverage, but I thought it was worth a try.

As I filled out the application my agent had sent me, I paused at the question asking me to list unusual hobbies. Finally I wrote: *I take long voyages in small boats on the open ocean.*

In a couple of weeks, my agent called me.

"Sorry," he said, "but we can't get you additional coverage without a big rate increase. You're a risk, you know."

I said nothing, but I could feel my heart thumping.

"After all," he continued, "you have a history of ulcers."

Now that was ironic. Apparently ocean voyages were acceptable but ulcers weren't.

As soon as the weather permitted, I began reworking the outside of the boat. I rebuilt the hatch cover, since the original plywood had started to delaminate. I also designed a new rudder because the old one was too hard to turn. The new one would, I hoped, be sufficiently balanced that the pressure of the water would take over part of the physical effort needed for steering.

I stowed another sea anchor, this one a parachute. Last year *Yankee Girl* had refused to lie to a small sea anchor, and I had kept buying bigger and bigger ones. In a 30 m.p.h. wind with one-and-a-half-foot waves, she would take a 30-inch sea anchor—which theoretically should hold a 25-foot boat—and run with it. She would pass right by the anchor, lift it to one side, and then start towing it. She was a stubborn little girl, and for this trait I almost started calling her the Yankee Brat.

By now most of White Bear's residents were becoming accustomed to my activities, but I always managed to take
someone by surprise. One day I went down to Larry's Live
Bait Shop and ordered ten spark plugs for my four-horsepower Evinrude. The mechanic was astounded.

"We rent these motors out all season and only change the
plugs once a year, unless there's something wrong," he said,
shaking his head.

"I'm taking a long trip," I confessed.

For a moment I thought that he was actually going to re-
fuse to sell me the spark plugs. But finally he wiped his oily
hands on his overalls and sighed.

"Okay, if you want 'em," he said. Then he helped me carry
them and some other gear, including a case of oil and a landing net, out to my car.

"Where are you going?" he asked casually as we loaded up
my station wagon.

Thoughts raced through my mind. I had been keeping my
journey a secret so far; only a few people knew about it.
Should I tell him? Well, why not?

"England," I replied. Then I waited for my grand announcement to sink in.

"Have a good trip," he said absentmindedly. I watched him
turn and walk away.

By April I knew that I would simply have to stop collecting
things and get going. My pilot charts told me that I'd have to
leave on June 1 in order to take advantage of the best winds.
After that date the winds were supposed to stay favorable for
most of the summer.

I began packing in earnest, making sometimes painful decisions about what I'd absolutely have to take and what I'd have
to leave behind. Toward the end of my packing, Sally came
out to see what I was doing.

"You may want to leave some of this stuff here and take
along more fishing gear," she said with a grin.

I didn't think that was so funny. She knows I hate fish.

By the middle of April I still had many items left over. Crossing my fingers, I started cramming them into the rear of the station wagon. I'd just have to try to fit them in later.

Then one evening I got out my pile of road maps and spread them on the table in front of me.

It would be a long drive to the East Coast, and I would make it alone.

IV

En Route to the Atlantic

"To him whose . . . thought
keeps pace with the sun,
the day is a perpetual morning."
Henry David Thoreau

Rain pelted down on the windshield of my station wagon as I droned eastward. Behind was my homemade trailer carrying *Yankee Girl*. Strapped down securely, she rested on a cushion of plywood chocks, her mast tied to the bed of the trailer.

I was finally on my way to the Atlantic.

Due to packing problems, my departure had been delayed three times. But at 7 A.M. on Wednesday, April 25—right after Sally had driven off to work—I had climbed into the car and pulled out of the driveway. There was something very comforting about that sequence of events. I felt as if Sally had left for her job, and now I was leaving for mine.

Our parting had even been a little businesslike.

"See you on the East Coast in a few weeks," I'd said as I kissed her goodbye.

"Drive carefully," she'd responded, hurrying off. "I hope you can fit everything in when you get there."

The day was cloudy, but that was fine with me; I'd rather drive in overcast than in glare. Within hours, though, it began to rain, and now it seemed as if the rain was going to follow me all the way.

I was heading for Virginia. After four months of agonizing over where to begin my journey, I'd settled on Chesapeake Bay.

The customary departure point for transatlantic crossings is Cape Cod, but that just didn't seem right for me and *Yankee Girl*. Leaving from there would mean that I'd have to cross both the New York and Boston shipping lanes, increasing my chances of being run down. I'd be within the iceberg limit for a longer period of time, and I'd probably encounter a number of foggy days.

In addition, the water and air are colder there than they are to the south, and Cape Cod is further away from the Gulf Stream than I wanted to be at the outset. On my way to the Stream I'd have to pass through the Grand Banks fishing fleets with their trawlers and nets. Finally, if anything went wrong and I had to cut my trip short, the only logical places to go would be Nova Scotia or Newfoundland—both of which have dangerous coastlines.

For a while I'd considered setting sail out of Jacksonville, Florida, but that didn't seem like a good idea either. All things considered, I felt that the route from Virginia would be the fastest and safest—even though it would also be about 300 miles longer. If my calculations proved correct, I'd be able to make up the extra miles within the first two weeks as a result of entering the Gulf Stream more quickly.

I was satisfied with my decision. I had arrived at it careful-

ly and after a great deal of thought. Now I just wanted to get
to Chesapeake Bay as soon as possible.

To save money while driving, I planned to spend the nights
on an air mattress in the back of my station wagon. But that
wasn't as easy as I thought it would be. The car was full of
gear, and before I could stretch out I had to toss most of it
into the front seat. Then, on my first night on the road, I
made the mistake of trying to sleep at a truck stop. I was
awakened every couple of hours by the noise of heavy diesels
as the truckers came and went.

In the morning I was tired and grumpy. I wasn't prepared
to face the problem of where to sleep. I'd need to be rested
when I arrived in Virgina, since the truly exhausting part of
my journey would begin there. I couldn't count on finding
campgrounds along the way, and I didn't want to incur the
additional expense. Where could I sleep undisturbed—and for
free?

On the second night I pulled into a shopping center in Fred-
erick, Maryland. I went inside, ate supper, browsed through a
bookstore, and washed up in a bathroom. As I walked back
out into the parking lot, the thought suddenly occurred to me:
why not sleep here? At night, shopping center parking lots are
as peaceful as graveyards.

Pleased with my discovery, I almost didn't notice the man
who was standing on the trailer and peering in at one of *Yankee Girl*'s small portholes.

"What *is* this thing?" he asked me, thinking that I too had
wandered over out of curiosity.

I decided to play along.

"It must be some kind of sailboat," I offered helpfully.

"Nope, that ain't no sailboat," he insisted.

"Well, what do *you* think it is?" I asked, leading him on.

He paused for a moment and then announced, "It's a submarine."

With her tiny portholes and stubby cabin, *Yankee Girl* did

look a bit like a submarine. I let the comment pass.

"It's from Minnesota," I remarked, pointing to my license plate.

"But what's it doing out here?" the man wanted to know.

"Beats me," I said. "But whatever it is," I added defensively, "it sure looks sturdy."

He walked off to his car, shaking his head.

It had been raining the whole time we'd been talking, and I shivered slightly. Tonight I'd have to sleep with my clothes on in a cold berth.

I hunkered down into my sleeping bag and thought about Sally and home. About now she'd be finishing up supper. I'd be seeing her again before too long, and already I could hardly wait. We'd planned for her to join me in Virginia for a short visit before I left; she'd be bringing any last-minute gear and some more beef jerky.

It was still raining in the morning. I got up early and had breakfast in the car: milk, granola, and a can of peaches. Afterward I took the gear I'd thrown into the front seat and put it in the back once more.

Sooner or later, everything in the car would have to fit inside *Yankee Girl*. I hadn't yet figured out how I was going to squeeze so much stuff into her tiny hull. There were plastic containers of various sizes—red ones for gasoline, large and small white ones for provisions. There were two rudders, the old one and the new one, along with fiberglass cloth, resin, and my grinder in case I wanted to make any modifications on the new one. There was *Yankee Girl*'s boom, which I'd made out of an ordinary two-by-four piece of lumber, and three sail bags, not to mention two sea anchors—the large 36-inch one and the even larger parachute.

All of these items were in addition to the air mattresses, cushions, pieces of lumber, tools, paints, solvents, spare parts, cleaning equipment, charts, and bags of magazines I was sure I couldn't do without on my journey.

The old wagon was heavily loaded, and so was *Yankee Girl.* The only spaces in her that hadn't already been packed full were the bilges. In them I'd store the food, gas, and water I'd buy in Virginia.

I knew that, once there, I'd face an ordeal of packing and repacking, unpacking and packing again. Some things would have to be left behind; of that I was sure. I just hoped that none of them would prove to be vital. I still had nightmares of getting out onto the Atlantic, desperately needing some small item, and not having it on board.

If that happened, I would have nowhere to turn for help. No boats would be following me, no planes would be flying overhead to check on me or rescue me if I had problems. Except for a few close friends, no one would even know when I left.

I was determined to be totally self-sufficient and self-contained. I only hoped that I wasn't asking too much of myself.

Before leaving Minnesota, I shared three "last suppers" with Sally and some of our friends. There was only supposed to be one "last supper," of course, but I had such a problem getting packed that there ended up being three.

The first was a "last pizza" dinner on Friday, April 13. Any comments people wanted to make about that particular date went unsaid.

On the following Friday, Sally and I went over to Barb and Gerry Beutel's house for a "last spaghetti" feast. I was supposed to leave on Monday morning, but I wasn't ready even then, so on that night everyone came over to our house for a third "last supper."

By now the ritual of saying goodbye was becoming quite a joke.

"This is the *last* last supper, isn't it?" Barb Beutel quipped.

"Yes, it is," I answered firmly. Then I leaned back from the table and grinned.

"Imagine—you'll all be stuck here in icy Minnesota, and I'll be enjoying an ocean cruise. I'll think of you while I'm drifting along on the Gulf Stream, getting a tan. . . ."

"Maybe we'll airdrop you a pizza," Barb interrupted.

"Just make sure it's hot," I said.

As my friends were leaving, Gerry handed me a little plaque with a prayer mounted on it: *Oh Lord, thy sea is so big and my boat is so small.*

"This goes with me," I promised. Later I would hang it inside *Yankee Girl*, near the center bulkhead where I'd be sure to see it often.

Bill Mezzano, who had believed in me and my project from the very beginning, also had a special gift for me. It was a radio that could pick up both AM and shortwave, and it had belonged to his father. I had spent several unsuccessful months looking for this type of radio; I knew it would be useful for direction finding and for checking the accuracy of my watches.

"This radio means a lot to me," Bill said as we stood at the door. "I don't mind loaning it to you, but I want it back when you come home."

"I'll take care of it," I promised.

It was good to know that he expected to see me again.

All along the route to the coast, I kept meeting people who had mistaken notions about my little girl. I could feel myself becoming more and more defensive.

At a tollbooth on the Pennsylvania Turnpike, the man inside leaned out to stare at *Yankee Girl*.

"What's that—a submarine?" he wanted to know.

Back to that old line.

"Yes, it is," I lied. I was tired of making explanations.

"I thought so," he said, pleased with himself.

The miles slipped by. Washington, D.C. Jamestown, Virginia. Newport News.

Newport News is the home of a famous mariner's museum, and I decided to visit it as I passed through. I drove over one morning at 8:30 A.M. and sat in the parking lot, waiting for the museum to open. I was having my usual breakfast of granola and milk when an old Ford pulled up alongside.

A red-faced man wearing a baseball cap rolled down his window and scrutinized me and my boat. Then his black eyes darted back to me.

"You going to sail that thing across the Atlantic?" he asked.

I was amazed. Most people I'd met hadn't even recognized that *Yankee Girl* was a sailboat. This man not only knew what she was, but he also knew what I was planning to do with her.

"She's capable of it," I answered guardedly.

"Then you must have come to see the *Little One*," he said. "She's inside."

Again I was amazed. The *Little One* was the boat that had belonged to William Willis, the famous single-hander. I had read about them both. She was only 11½ feet long—a foot and a half longer than *Yankee Girl*. In her Willis had tried three times to cross the Atlantic from west to east, the same feat I was about to attempt. Twice he had been picked up at sea, but on his third voyage the *Little One* had been spotted by a freighter only 400 miles off the Irish coast—and Willis had not been on board. No one ever found out what had happened to him; he had simply disappeared at sea.

And here was his boat, in a museum I had stopped at on a whim.

The man drove off and I finished my breakfast. When the museum opened, I was the first visitor inside. I found the *Little*

One in a far corner, surrounded by railings and covered with a layer of dust.

I was awestruck.

After quickly looking around to make sure I was alone, I climbed under the fence and, by standing on another railing, was able to peer inside her.

As I touched her battered transom, I thought about William Willis, that grand old man of the sea who'd refused to give up. In the end, he had become part of the sea.

I could see that the *Little One* had suffered a lot of damage. Her mast and boom were gone, a chainplate had been sheared off at the deck, and bare wood was exposed in several places where the fiberglass had been torn away. Part of her keel was also broken.

From my reading I knew that the *Little One* had started out as a 21-foot sailing sloop with an open cockpit. Willis had cut her down to 11½ feet by chopping off her bow and transom. Then he had added a cabin so he could steer from the inside—not unlike the arrangement I had on *Yankee Girl*.

To my eyes, she was not a bad boat at all. Despite the extensive modifications Willis had made to her hull, she looked strong. And she had survived the Atlantic, even though Willis had not.

I stared into her cabin, transfixed. Questions crowded my mind. What had happened to Willis? Had he slipped overboard? Had he fallen into such a deep depression that he'd taken his own life? Why hadn't he kept a log—or, if he had, why had no one found it?

And would *Yankee Girl* and I suffer the same fate?

Willis had been only one of many who'd disappeared at sea. In 1966, two Englishmen named David Johnston and John Hoare had attempted to row across the Atlantic from Virginia Beach. Months later their boat had been found floating upside-down, their log still inside. Johnston and Hoare were never seen again.

Footsteps sounded behind me, and my reverie ended. I scrambled back to the other side of the railing and walked away, leaving the *Little One* to gather more dust.

Outside in the parking lot, *Yankee Girl* was a welcome sight. I brightened as soon as I saw her jaunty blue-and-green hull.

"You look great," I said, patting her side affectionately. "And I know we're going to make it."

When I arrived at Virginia Beach, I drove to several marinas looking for a slip. Finally, at Lynnhaven Municipal Marina, I found one of the few transient spaces available.

"How much?" I asked the operator.

"Twenty cents a foot," he replied. "How big is your boat?"

"Ten feet," I said.

"Well, then, you'll get by pretty cheaply," he noted with a smile.

I was elated. I'd been worrying about where I'd put in, and now I had my very own slip—number 31. I was all set.

I wanted to clean *Yankee Girl* up before launching her, so I drove around town until I found a coin-operated car wash. Then I sudsed her off and gave her a good coat of paste wax.

It was time to get down to the business of buying food, water, and gasoline. I unloaded what gear I could from the station wagon, packed it into the boat, and headed for the nearest grocery store.

My shopping trip took me three days, and I had to go to three separate supermarkets before I found enough distilled water. As I pulled up to one checkout counter with a cart containing nothing but ten gallons of water, I got some very strange looks.

I bought a total of 450 cans of food, including everything

from asparagus to stew, chili to Chinese foods, soups to juices. I must have filled the back end of my station wagon half a dozen times.

At one store I visited, the employees were just finishing taking inventory. After loading up my cart with 12 cans of Dinty Moore stew—their entire stock—and all of their chicken ala king, I noticed an employee staring at me incredulously, notepad in hand. When I reached the cash register, the girl there yelled out to her friend in the aisle, "Hey, Mildred! You should have waited until this guy went through. Now you'll have to take inventory all over again!"

Yankee Girl had nine separate compartments below her waterline. They varied in capacity, but each was more or less wedge-shaped—broad at the top and narrower toward the keel. The gasoline went into the forward lockers, and the food and water were distributed throughout the rest of the boat. I had been careful to buy water in plastic jugs with strong screw caps, but I stored them upright anyway just in case; I didn't want any leakage below the deck.

Cans were put in sideways and stacked. One locker, for example, was about a foot deep, measured 2 feet by 2 feet at the top, and narrowed down toward the keel. Into it went five rows of 17 cans each, or 85 cans.

As I packed, unpacked, and repacked my little boat, I discovered additional nooks and crannies. I stored even more cans in these. In fact, I was able to add another 90 to my original supply, giving me a total of 540.

At last *Yankee Girl* carried enough weight to be launched safely. But I had an 1,800-pound load on a trailer designed to carry only 1,200. With the springs on the trailer creaking under the strain, I drove carefully to a dry storage marina.

"How much to launch her?" I asked the manager, hoping for a break.

"Normally we ask $1 a foot," he said, sizing up the tiny hull. "But your boat is so small that we'll have to charge $2 a foot." Then he signaled to two husky youths. They ambled over, grinning.

"Holy mackerel," one of them said as he struggled to lift *Yankee Girl*'s bow. "What've you got in this thing?" He had stopped grinning.

At this yard, launching involved three steps: hoisting a boat onto a forklift's sling, transferring it via forklift to an elevator, and then lowering it into the water. The young men obviously thought that, given *Yankee Girl*'s size, they could skip a step or two. But no matter how much the two of them grunted, they couldn't budge her bow.

With a lot of shoving and the aid of the forklift, they finally managed to get *Yankee Girl* into the sling. Then, bypassing the elevator, they lowered her directly into the water.

They had charged me double, and they hadn't even used the elevator, but at least *Yankee Girl* was safely launched. I jumped aboard, waved them off, and turned toward the marina.

The first thing I did when I arrived at my slip was to step the mast. I would be spending the next several days living and sleeping on board *Yankee Girl*.

On one side of me was a 33-foot Egg Harbor Sedan, and on the other was a 31-foot Bertram Flying Bridge Sport Fisherman. Sandwiched between the two of them, *Yankee Girl* looked like a toy.

It wasn't long before I started hearing the standard jokes and gibes about my little girl. One morning, as I was waking up, three fishermen strolled by.

"What the heck is that thing?" one asked.

"That's the weirdest boat I've ever seen," said another.

I opened the hatch, yawned, stretched, and glared at them. Immediately one of them walked over.

"We didn't know you were in there," he apologized. "We didn't mean anything disrespectful to your boat. It's just that we've never seen anything like it."

"That's all right," I replied. "It's a miniature cruising sailboat. I trailered her out from Minnesota to do a little sailing on the bay."

That seemed to satisfy their curiosity.

Another comment I heard more times than I cared to count was, "Where's the rest of your boat?" By now I'd come up with an answer that usually put an end to that conversation: "My wife and I are divorced, and she has the other half."

Some people began to speculate openly about my sleeping arrangements. A few even invited me to stay at their homes, where, according to them, I could "get at least one good night's sleep."

But one couple, Sam and Anne Murphey, sincerely wanted to help, and we soon became close friends.

"Why don't you come and stay at our house?" asked Sam, a retired Navy pilot. Anne nodded her agreement.

"I'm sleeping fine," I replied. "But there is one thing I don't have: a shower."

"You can use ours anytime," they told me.

I started seeing the Murpheys every evening. Old Fred, their beagle, made sure of that. He liked his nightly walk, and if he didn't think he was going to get it he'd set up a mournful baying. Whenever I heard his howls, I knew that Sam and Anne would soon be by for a visit.

I found two more new friends in Jack Lewis, the captain of a 65-foot research vessel named *The Pathfinder*, and his wife, Virginia. Jack showed me where he kept the key to his boat and told me that I could come aboard for a shower or a rest as often as I liked.

I spent the early part of May packing and repacking. An unexpected problem had surfaced: I was smelling gas fumes. Twice I had taken all of the gasoline containers out of the bilges and checked them for leaks, but I had not been able to find any. I was afraid that the fumes would make me sick; I was also worried about the possibility of an explosion. Even though the containers seemed secure, the odor persisted.

By now the working sails—the main and the two jibs—had been bent on and secured along the boom and on the bow, with their bags stowed below. The 180-square-foot spinnaker was secured up forward for use later on. Other than these, I would carry no "extra" sails.

I had made some final decisions as to what I would and wouldn't take along on my voyage. The 18- and 36-inch sea anchors would come with me, but the parachute would go back to Minnesota. I'd realized that if I ever did need to deploy the parachute, it would be a big soggy mess afterward, and I'd never be able to get it back inside *Yankee Girl*'s tiny cabin.

I also decided against my landing net, pistol, and spear gun. I packed a few pieces of plywood for emergency repairs, but most of the lumber I'd brought to Virginia would stay there. That left space in the boat for my assortment of screws and bolts, the riveter, saws, a brace and bits, a hatchet, files, a crowbar, and clamps.

Before leaving Minnesota I'd stashed 22 pounds of lead ballast in my station wagon, and now I wasn't sure what to do with it. I spent hours putting it in the boat, taking it out, and putting it in again. But as I stored more and more supplies aboard *Yankee Girl*, I could see that she was really getting loaded down. So I stuck to my original concept of not taking any "dead weight" to sea, and the lead ended up back in the car once and for all.

When I had finished loading everything but fresh foods— I'd do that just before I left—I sat back and reflected on what I'd accomplished so far.

I was pleased. *Yankee Girl* was turning out to be a splendid little ocean-going cruiser. She was holding more supplies than I'd ever thought possible; in fact, I'd been able to add to my original allotments of both gasoline and food. With what she was carrying in her hull, I could last far longer than 90 days at sea.

I'd done everything I could to ensure that my expedition

would be well-designed, well-planned, and well-equipped. The way things were going, it would also be one of the least expensive ever launched. To date I had spent a total of $2,924—all of it out of my own pocket. Most of the $1,000 I'd added since my last cost accounting had gone for extra compasses, anchors, strobe lights, charts, and radios. I now had no fewer than five radios on board.

As the day of my departure drew nearer, I started worrying about whether I'd forgotten anything important. My new friends, the Murpheys, were eager to help in whatever way they could. One evening they invited me to dinner, and Anne introduced a modified game of "20 Questions" that we'd continue to play for the next several days.

"Have you got a spare can opener?" she would ask.

"I'm bringing two," I'd reply after checking my mental list.

"What if your matches get wet?" Sam would inquire. "How will you light your stove?"

"They're sealed in an airtight jar, and I'll be carrying three cigarette lighters, a flint igniter, and spare flints."

The game went on, but the Murpheys were never able to catch me with a question I couldn't answer.

The time had come to do some sailing with my fully loaded craft. I especially wanted to try out my new rudder. So I decided to take a cruise to Tangier Island, about 55 miles up Chesapeake Bay.

On the morning when I was preparing to cast off, a few of the dock loungers came by.

"Going for a sail?" one of them asked.

"Just up to Tangier," I answered casually.

"It can get pretty rough out there," another said.

I could tell that they all had serious doubts about me and my boat, but I wasn't in the mood for a discussion. I kept on working until they finally ambled off.

At 9 A.M. I passed through Lynnhaven Inlet. Chesapeake Bay stretched out ahead of me for more than 100 miles. Fortunately the bay was calm today—so calm, in fact, that I had to motor for the first three hours. Chesapeake may be shallow, but if the winds are right she can kick up some steep waves.

I was determined to make Tangier in record time, so I sailed until 2 A.M., stopping only once to wait out the ebb tide. I anchored for the rest of the night and entered the narrow channel by daylight. After lunch and a brief tour of the island, I headed back down the western shore.

There the winds were much stronger. Faced with five-foot waves, I had the opportunity to thoroughly test *Yankee Girl* and her new rudder. Neither disappointed me. My chunky little girl took the waves in stride, and the new rudder proved easier to steer than the old one; all it required was finger pressure.

I sailed across the bay to Cape Charles and spent my next night in harbor. It rained on my way back to Lynnhaven, and that gave me the chance to check out both the self-steering mechanism and my poncho. Here I discovered some minor problems. The self-steering suffered from too much friction on the sheets, and my poncho kept the wind out but let the rain through.

Despite these and other things that needed correcting, I was satisfied. Loaded down as she was, my tiny boat was performing beautifully.

When I arrived back at the marina, my dockside acquaintances came up to gloat.

"Ever make it to Tangier?" one of them asked with a grin.

"I got there the first night," I answered. I had to suppress a smile when I saw their reaction; a few jaws actually dropped.

"Beginners' luck," I heard one mutter as they shuffled off down the dock. "He must have caught the tide just right."

News travels fast. After that some of the regulars at Lynnhaven gave me and *Yankee Girl* a bit more respect. I tried to ignore the others as I prepared for Sally's visit.

I had rented a rustic cabin in the woods near the beach. We'd spend a few days there relaxing together.

I met her at the airport. She was carrying her suitcase and an enormous box filled with more beef jerky, some granola, and a new poncho she'd sewn for me.

"I never want to see beef jerky again for as long as I live," she said, thrusting the box at me. She wrinkled her nose in disgust.

That I could understand. In my absence she had "jerked" 60 pounds of raw beef down to about 300 ounces of dried meat. The smell in the house must have been intolerable.

In minutes we were headed for the cabin in my old station wagon. For the next five days we sunbathed, read, and strolled barefoot along the beach, looking for shells and watching the birds circle overhead. I caught Sally staring out at the sea more than once, but we both tried to avoid talking about my journey. Instead we focused on the present and just enjoyed being together.

"It's nice to be alone with you," I said to her one evening as we walked through the pines behind the cabin.

"I wish it could last forever," she answered wistfully.

We were silent for a few minutes.

"Your parents must have a lot of confidence in you," Sally noted, changing the subject. "If they were really worried, they'd be out here too."

That took me by surprise. I had been thinking that my parents had stayed home to give Sally and me a chance to be together. But their motives had been more profound than that. By remaining in Minnesota instead of coming out to see me, they had been expressing their support and reassurance. Realizing this gave me a tremendous psychological boost.

I would think a lot about Sally and my parents in the lonely weeks ahead. Their love would be a constant source of strength for me.

All too soon, our vacation came to an end. It was nearly the end of May, and in order to meet my schedule I'd have to leave in a few short days. As I drove Sally to the airport for her return trip, the atmosphere in the car grew tense. We both knew that we wouldn't be seeing each other again for a long time.

Our final conversation at the gate was strained.

"If you need anything, call Dad or Bill Mezzano," I said.

"I will," Sally replied evenly.

"Try to remember to keep your gas tank filled up, okay?" I asked, making an attempt at humor. She had a habit of driving around with her gas gauge needle on empty.

"I'll be fine," she said. She was avoiding my eyes.

"I'll see you in England before you know it," I went on, trying to cheer her up. "We'll go to one of those old hotels by the sea and have a little holiday."

It was time for her to go, and we held each other tightly for a moment more. Suddenly I felt her shoulders shaking. She was crying.

"I can't help it," she said, her voice muffled against my shoulder. "I'm entitled to cry if I want to."

"You know there isn't anything to worry about." I said, patting her back.

"I'm just afraid that if anything happened to you. . . ."

Her voice trailed off. Then she pulled away from me and looked down at the floor.

"Ger, I wouldn't be able to make it on my own."

I put my arms around her again and tried to collect my thoughts. Then I noticed a little boy in cowboy boots standing off to one side. He had obviously been staring at us.

"Someone's looking our way," I told Sally, nodding in his direction. She couldn't help but smile when she saw the expression on his chubby face.

"We're going to ruin his day if we keep going on like this," I joked.

That did it. She let go of me and picked up her bag.

"I'll be waiting for you in England," she said. Then she

turned and walked down the long, empty corridor, a slim figure clutching a shoulder bag. For a moment I was tempted to
join her—to go back to Minnesota, to the peace and security
of home.

I watched her until she turned a corner and was gone.

My last days in port were busy ones. I checked and rechecked
everything on the boat and the rigging and added two turning
blocks to reduce the friction on the jib sheets. I also bought
two more grocery carts full of fruit and 60 eggs to add to the
half-dozen I already had on board. Before packing the eggs
away, I smeared each with Vaseline and replaced it carefully
in its carton. Shielding them from the sea air would, I hoped,
help them to last longer.

Yankee Girl was squatting down on her lines, filled from
stem to stern with provisions. I was determined not to be
caught short on anything.

I spent my last night on shore at the Murpheys'. I went
over to their house late in the afternoon; they had offered to
store my car and trailer for me while I was gone, and I wanted to get the trailer moved before dinner. Sam came out to
give me a hand at unhitching it, and slowly we began pushing
it through his back yard.

"Are you sure this won't be in the way?" I asked Sam.

"No, we'll just put it in the back of the lot. There's plenty
of room," he answered.

As we walked by the side of the house, I noticed that old
Fred, the Murpheys' gray-muzzled beagle, was looking at me
with more than ordinary interest. All at once, growling like a
puppy, he charged. He scurried between Sam's legs and made
a grab for my pants.

"Fred, get out of here!" Sam hollered.

But Fred had a grip on my cuff, and he wasn't about to let go. I was in a real dilemma: if I dropped the trailer to defend myself, it would land right on top of Fred.

It was a standoff.

Wondering what all the growling and shouting was about, Anne had appeared at a window. When she saw what old Fred was up to, she ran out of the house and grabbed him.

"I'm going to give you a couple of whacks," she threatened as she pried him away from me.

"I thought that dog knew me by now," I said, rubbing my leg.

Fortunately I was unscratched. But if Fred had succeeded in biting me, that would have been the end of my voyage. I couldn't have gone to sea if there had been any chance of infection.

What a close call! Two years of hard work had almost gone down the drain—all because of an old sea dog's nip.

Later that evening, as I said goodbye to my shoreside friends, Tom Ellis surprised me by presenting me with a barometer he'd used for many years in the Venezuelan jungles. And Sam loaned me the signal mirror he'd been carrying when he was shot down over Korea.

"I want this back," Sam gruffly insisted, reminding me of what Bill Mezzano had said at the end of our last "last supper" in Minnesota.

Throughout the evening, my friends were careful to keep me in the right frame of mind. They knew how essential psychological preparation could be to a lone sailor. All during the month of May, I had kept up my mental conditioning—thinking positively and maintaining a sense of optimism. That was turning out to be just as important as any of the other preparations I'd made.

That night I telephoned my parents and friends back home to say goodbye.

"We'll be with you all the way," my mother reassured me.

"Don't get my radio wet," Bill said.

The last person I called was Sally. She began crying almost immediately.

"I need you," she kept repeating.

"Don't worry," I said, trying to comfort her. "We'll be together in England soon, and we'll have a wonderful time there."

She was still crying when we both hung up.

After that I had to fight a growing depression. I knew that Sally had tried to hold her feelings back, and we had talked often about what the trip would mean to us. But everything had broken down in the end.

I slept lightly that night. The words that no one had dared to speak crowded my mind.

There was always the possibility that I wouldn't make it.

V

Casting Off for England

"Don't be afraid to take a big
step if one is indicated.
You can't cross a chasm
in two small jumps."
David Lloyd George

A steady breeze blew out of the southwest as *Yankee Girl* sliced purposefully through Chesapeake Bay. Rigged under twin jibs and riding the ebb tide, she ran through the light swells easily and with grace.

It was Friday, June 1, 1979, and my transatlantic crossing had begun.

I had the satisfaction of knowing that I'd cast off on the best day of the year for such a voyage. The spring storms were over, and hurricanes usually didn't start appearing until later in the summer. If the weather followed its normal seasonal pattern, I'd have favorable winds during the weeks ahead, winds that would boost me along to England.

As the Chesapeake light slid by to starboard, I breathed a word of thanks for the breeze that was carrying me quickly out to sea and away from the hazards of the coast.

It was then the realization finally hit home: *I was alone in a ten-foot boat facing 3,800 miles of open ocean.*

I had spent years preparing for this moment, but somehow it still took me by surprise. *Yankee Girl* and I were as ready as we could ever be. She was in perfect shape and loaded down with more provisions than I could possibly need. I was in good physical and psychological condition. I had taken every precautionary measure I could think of, planning my trip down to the tiniest detail in order to decrease the number of unknowns. But there was one unknown remaining that I could do nothing about: the sea itself.

The Chesapeake light would be the last fixed structure I'd see until I reached England. I turned my attention back to the rusty old platform, burning it into my memory, and kept looking over my shoulder at it until it sank beneath the horizon.

I had now been on the water for about six hours. Six hours out of 60 days—assuming all went well.

A few of my friends and some of the people from the marina were on hand when I cast off in the early morning hours. I hadn't really wanted them to come, but they had insisted.

The day dawned gloomy and overcast, and there was a threat of rain in the air. The leaden skies made me feel more tired than I'd been when I'd climbed out of bed. I had spent the night rolling and tossing about, unable to catch more than an hour of sleep at a time. This was in spite of the fact that I had been in a real bed; the Murpheys had insisted that I spend the night with them. It was the last chance I'd have to stretch out for a long time.

When I did manage to slip off to sleep, I was plagued by

bad dreams. I had forgotten something; I had lost my way; I was being run down by a ship. That last dream was the worst. Again and again I envisioned a black hull coming at me like a steel wall, blind to me and my tiny boat.

I was awakened by old Fred, who was performing his usual morning concert of barking at the mallards that had settled in the yard during the night.

"How about some bacon and eggs?" Sam inquired brightly, poking his head into my room.

"Just a bowl of cornflakes would be fine," I answered, rubbing my eyes. But Sam was determined to send me off with a hearty breakfast. By the time I stumbled into the kitchen, he had fixed me not only the cereal I'd asked for but also toast, orange juice, and sausages.

"I'm sorry, Sam, but I can't eat all of this," I said. "I'm too nervous." I managed to down only half of my bowl of cereal.

I was at dockside by 6:30 A.M., eager to be off and catch the tide. First, though, I had some last-minute packing to do. Somehow I stuffed two more carts of fresh foods on board. Then I stowed my sack of books and 40 back issues of *Reader's Digest*. Considering the months I'd be spending at sea, it would have been a serious oversight to forget my reading materials.

"Are you leaving any room for yourself?" one friend asked half-seriously.

I paused, holding the last of five bags of grapefruit I was attempting to stuff into the cabin. It *was* getting pretty crowded in there.

"I guess I'll just have to eat my way in," I noted glumly.

More people were gathering on the dock, watching me in silence. Occasionally someone tried to make a joke, but in general the mood was not very cheerful. Although everyone had come intending to wish me bon voyage, they stood there like mourners at a funeral, heads bent and hands at their sides.

I had to be careful not to let their feelings affect me. This was not the time to start thinking negative thoughts.

"Any last words?" someone asked. Then he looked away in embarrassment.

That did it. I almost expected one of them to step forward and lay a wreath across *Yankee Girl*'s cabin top.

Finally I handed my mooring lines to Sam.

"Don't expect to hear from me for at least two weeks," I reminded him. "I'll try to get a message back to you, but don't worry about me—and don't ever report me missing. I may not be able to contact you until I get to the other side."

He nodded. He knew almost as much about my trip as I did, for I had given him a copy of my Float Plan. It listed all of the information required by the Coast Guard for boats going offshore, including descriptions of my boat, myself, and the safety equipment I was carrying, my intended route, and my estimated time of arrival.

I yanked on the starting cord and the Evinrude sputtered to life. As I headed out of the marina, I glanced at my watch. It was 7:30 A.M.; I was already running an hour and a half behind schedule. I'd have to hurry to get out of the capes before the tide turned against me.

I didn't look back until I'd left the people on the dock far behind.

The Chesapeake light had barely sunk over the horizon when the moist southwest wind died and sunlight pierced through the clouds.

The sails slatted as *Yankee Girl* rolled. The air had become perfectly still. I had tried sailing for a while, but now there wasn't even a breath of wind. I'd have to start up my motor again or the tide would carry me back into the bay.

It was going to be a very hot day, and I was already uncomfortable in my heavy clothing. I pulled off my white wool sweater and pants and sealed them in a plastic bag. If all went according to plan I'd put them on again, still fresh and clean, when I reached England.

Then I buckled my safety harness over my T-shirt. I would wear it throughout the entire voyage. From now on *Yankee Girl* and I would be one.

To protect myself from the sun's intense rays, I put on a long-sleeved shirt and a pair of shorts and smeared myself with suntan lotion. As a final touch, I donned my pith helmet. Leaving the slatting mainsail up for shade, I reached over and started the motor. It caught with a rasp, and we were soon on our way at a steady three knots.

Before long the temperature climbed to over 90 degrees and I began to perspire. The light glinting off the surface of the water was blinding, and I reached for my sunglasses. Over these I clipped a second pair of dark lenses.

I was sitting on my little tiller seat, sipping my first can of apple juice and enjoying the view, when I felt a stinging pain.

I looked down to see a large black fly perched on my right leg. As I swatted it, I peered into the cabin. A half-dozen more were buzzing around my provisions. Grabbing my can of insect repellent, I sprayed everything in sight. Then, while I was congratulating myself on my speed and efficiency, I jumped. Another fly had bitten my bare leg.

I had expected a few stowaways, but I hadn't counted on being the only landing spot in this part of the ocean. For the next eight hours I held the tiller in one hand and the bug spray in the other, fending off the flies that came from miles around to snack on me.

As I scratched my bites and sighed, I realized how tired I really was. I hoped that I'd be able to get some sleep soon, for I needed it badly. Precisely *where* I'd sleep was a problem I hadn't yet solved, though. *Yankee Girl* was stuffed full of provisions from transom to forepeak.

Even the footwell, which I'd designed in such a way that I could sit with my feet down, was packed with eight two-gallon containers of gasoline. I'd decided at the last minute to bring my gasoline supply up to 60 gallons, and sacrificing a bit more cabin space had seemed worth it at the time. But now I wasn't sure.

Since my butane stove was meant to hang from a bracket above the footwell, I wouldn't be able to cook on it until I'd used up those 16 gallons of gas. Otherwise the danger of an explosion would be too great. Given the size of my outboard, though, that could take days. Meanwhile I'd have to sit cross-legged—and eat cold food.

I looked up at the sky. The light was beginning to fade. Hungry flies, a blazing sun, and stiff legs hadn't made the first day of my voyage very enjoyable. I wondered what the night would bring—and how much more discomfort I would face in the coming weeks.

Then I shook my head, hard. It was far too early to be thinking such thoughts. My problems seemed worse than they were simply because I was so tired. Things would look better in the morning—*if* I got some sleep.

I hadn't had any real rest for nearly 36 hours, and I knew from experience how dangerous this could be. On my second attempt at a major voyage five years earlier, my lack of physical preparation had nearly proved fatal. I'd left Miami and sailed nonstop for 33 hours, refusing to give myself time to rest. Finally I began to hallucinate. Unable to think straight or make reasoned decisions, I continued to battle adverse winds and waves for 50 more miles before giving up and turning back.

By 3 A.M. Miami was in sight, and I foolishly headed straight for the lights of the hotels along the beach. I didn't come to my senses until I was in the breakers. Desperately I fought my way back through the waves and sailed down the beach, searching for an inlet. An incredible 12 hours later I dropped anchor in the bay. By then I was so weak that when I tried to drink a cup of water I immediately vomited.

I had made it back safely, but I had been lucky. And I had

promised myself never to fall into that trap again.

Yet here I was, already on the brink of exhaustion, and this trip was an even greater challenge than the last one had been.

Only this time I would not turn back.

VI

Battle to the Gulf Stream

"Surely oak and threefold brass
surrounded his heart who first
trusted a frail vessel to
the merciless ocean."
Horace

 **I** slowly awoke for what seemed like the thousandth time. With each roll of the boat, the pain in my ribs and the cramps in my legs increased. I had been lying in a fetal position with my head forward, my legs under the tiller, and my feet up against the transom. Frustrated and exhausted, I sat up—and bumped my head against the bulkhead.

My first night at sea was not going according to plan.

Inside *Yankee Girl*'s tiny cabin, the air was stuffy and stale. Because of the heavy condensation that occurs at night, I had closed the hatch; it was either that or risk having everything saturated. But that had caused another problem: the smell of gasoline had become overpowering. My head was throbbing, and I was beginning to feel nauseated.

I understood what was causing my leg cramps—the lack of stretching room—but the pain in my ribs was a mystery. I felt as if I'd been lying on rocks. Groping around on the bunk, I discovered the cause of my discomfort: grapefruit. I had slept with three of them grinding into my ribs.

In my last-minute packing zeal, I had somehow squeezed five bags of grapefruit into the cabin. Now they were rolling everywhere.

It was still dark outside. Using my red flashlight, I checked my watch. It was only 1 A.M. I had been asleep on and off for about three hours.

What a miserable night!

Although I needed sleep—badly—I'd only been able to nap for 15 minutes at a stretch. Since I'd already spent many nights on board *Yankee Girl*, I'd thought that sleep would come easily. But dozing off in the middle of White Bear Lake was vastly different from going to sleep on the ocean. In Minnesota I hadn't had to worry about being run over by ships. Suddenly I was terrified that that might happen. I knew that a ship coming toward me in the misty darkness simply wouldn't see me in time.

I was also suffering from a mild claustrophobia. On more than one occasion during this night I'd awakened abruptly, gasping for breath.

Now I slid open the hatch, poked my head outside, and breathed deeply. The sea air felt good on my face and in my lungs. Slowly I tried to straighten up—and groaned. After hours of being coiled up like a spring, my back was stiff and sore.

I stared out over the undulating ocean. A sliver of a moon cast its pale light on the black water. I was alone with the sea, the moon, and the mist.

Once again I was aware of my terrible solitude.

I turned around in the hatch and surveyed the horizon.

Then, as if to justify my fears, a set of navigation lights appeared off my starboard bow. But where were they headed—toward me, or away from me? Dazed and confused, I waited with growing anxiety to see whether the red and green lights were coming closer. As I peered into the distance, trying to get a fix on the ship, *Yankee Girl* made matters worse by continuing to bob up and down.

It took a while, but I was finally able to determine that we were not on a collision course. The ship was moving north, possibly toward New York. Sighing in relief, I dropped back inside the cabin and began coping with the more immediate problem of rearranging grapefruit in the dark so I could lie down.

I soon realized that there isn't much one can do with a lot of loose grapefruit. I'd just have to lie on them—or eat them. At the moment I was too ill to do anything but collapse once more on my lumpy bed.

By dawn I was glad to get up, even though it was only 4:35 A.M. I threw open the hatch, peered out at the brightening sky, and stretched. Every muscle in my body screamed in protest.

I took stock of my situation: so far, not so good. This was only the beginning of my second day at sea, and already I was tired and sore. I had gotten very little sleep and almost no rest. Even the sea looked hostile and threatening; beneath the growing light, it was a sickening blend of magenta and purple.

I shivered. It was chilly at this hour. Then I became aware of something else that added to my unhappiness: there was no wind, not even a whisper.

Some sailors can sense wind on their cheeks, but I use my ears to detect the slightest breeze. I turned my head from left to right, alert to any pressure or air movement. Nothing.

Precisely at that moment a voice sounded inside my head.

"Last night you didn't want wind so you could sleep. Now you want wind so you can sail. Can't you make up your mind?"

I straightened in surprise. This was happening far sooner

than I'd expected. Still, it would have to be dealt with.

"You're early," I said easily.

My imaginary friend had arrived.

Like a parent awaiting a child's return, I had prepared for the coming of my imaginary friend. I had known all along that one of the greatest dangers of my voyage would be the utter loneliness I'd experience. In the absence of other human company, I would—either subconsciously or consciously—try to alleviate my solitude by "making up" a traveling companion.

I was not the only sailor who did this. Almost every single-hander ended up talking to himself at one time or another—and answering. The phenomenon was not at all unusual. But some imaginary friends were not necessarily friendly. I was determined that mine would be, so I welcomed him. I had to. I would hear his voice throughout my journey, and I didn't want it to turn hostile.

One famous sailor named Robert Manry came to believe that he had a mischievous elf on board who advised him to steer for a nonexistent island. Following the elf's directions, Manry zigzagged around the ocean for hours. Joshua Slocum, the first great single-hander, became convinced that Christopher Columbus's pilot was riding alongside him, urging him to turn around and set sail for Bermuda. Slocum gave in and only much later realized that he had gone miles off course.

I would not let my friend get the upper hand.

He had no name; he didn't need one. All during the crossing I would use him as a sounding board—talking to him and waiting for his replies, asking him for suggestions when I needed to make a decision, letting him cheer me up when I became discouraged. He would joke with me, encourage me, berate me, argue with me—and, above all, keep me mentally balanced. It sounded strange, but it was true. My friend would be my ace in the hole, my secret weapon. Though he was only a fabrication, a trick my mind was playing on itself, he would help to keep me alive in the months ahead.

Accepting the presence of my imaginary friend had allowed me to establish a sort of inner equilibrium. Suddenly I was ready to take action. I pumped up the fuel pressure bulb and yanked the starting cord. But when the Evinrude coughed and roared, I jumped. I had not expected it to make that much noise. After hours of hearing nothing but the stillness of the open sea and the slap-slap of the swells against *Yankee Girl's* hull, the sound of the motor was deafening.

I began motoring into the sunrise, and by about 6 A.M. a slight wind had arisen. It was coming out of the northeast: more bad news.

Leaving the motor running, I reached forward and quickly hoisted the jib and mainsail. The jib had been lying loosely on the foredeck, but it was already hanked onto the forestay. The mainsail had been lashed to the boom with shock cords.

They both went up easily and caught the wind. *Yankee Girl* veered off to the east-southeast—not in the direction I'd wanted her to go, but at least we were sailing. I would have preferred to continue due east on a course that would ultimately bring me to England, but this was the best we could do for now.

"Don't start complaining; you always wanted to see Africa," my imaginary friend teased.

"Well, then, maybe I will," I answered.

The wind continued to head me, and I motor-sailed through that day and part of the night. Finally, after 16 hours at the helm, I turned off the motor, dropped the sails, and closed the hatch.

In the dimness I tried to find something more substantial to eat than the oranges and granola bars I'd been snacking on during the day. But all I could manage to eat was a peanut butter and jelly sandwich washed down by a cup of water. It was as much as my stomach could tolerate at that point; I had not yet adjusted to the boat's constant motion.

I felt fine as long as I was above deck in the fresh air, but whenever I ducked my head below I became nauseated. Ignoring my queasiness, I lay down in *Yankee Girl*'s crowded cabin, determined to catch some sleep. The grapefruit hadn't gotten any softer during the past several hours, though. In fact, they seemed to have gotten harder. And bigger.

"Why don't you eat them?" my friend suggested.

My stomach lurched.

"That's a great idea," I responded, "but who's going to clean up the mess when I get sick? You?"

He didn't answer.

That made me feel better. Apparently I *would* have the last word with him—once in a while.

For the next 72 hours I followed the same routine: motor-sailing for 16 to 18 hours during the day and getting whatever rest I could at night. The waves weren't merely swells any longer; some of them were approaching five or six feet in height. I was traveling about the same distance vertically as I was horizontally.

Occasionally, out of sheer frustration, I would head due east. But then *Yankee Girl* would dive down the back of one wave and bury her bow in the next. Green water would roll up the deck to the base of the mast and we would shudder to a stop. It felt as if we were running into an enormous sponge.

Then I would have to head south for a while, giving *Yankee Girl* time to build up her momentum before turning east-southeast again. I had to battle for every mile of the way. I knew that if I let up for even a moment the headwinds and the currents would combine to drive me back to Cape Hatteras, the infamous "graveyard of the Atlantic."

Though the thermometer read 60 degrees, I was very cold.

My knees knocked against the tiller as I rolled from side to side on my little seat.

Because of my boat's tendency to plow downward into the waves, I had to hold on to the hatch coaming with both hands. To protect myself from the elements, I wore gloves and a down-filled jacket beneath my foul-weather gear. Shielding my head were my wool watch cap, my long-billed baseball cap, and the hood of my foul-weather jacket.

It felt exactly as if I were riding a teeter-totter in a 20-m.p.h. wind and someone was spraying me with a hose.

"Don't you love cruising?" my friend asked with a tinge of irony. "Isn't it just like the sailing magazines describe it?"

"Oh, I like it a lot," I quipped. "If only some of those yachting writers could be with us now!" The thought made me smile.

By my fourth day out I was starting to get desperate. The wind continued to blow straight out of the east, and I was still fighting the weather for hours at a stretch. In the meantime I was beginning to lose my powers of concentration—a bad sign.

I persisted in motoring as close to the east as possible, picking my way between the waves and steering as carefully as I could. The process was a tricky one: I had to slide eastward down each wave's slope and then head south-southeast before starting up the next one.

At night, when I went below to sleep, the motion of the sea and the pervasive smell of gasoline combined to keep me awake. Often I came close to vomiting. After those endless days at the helm, I was so exhausted that I had trouble unwinding. Usually I just lay down between piles of gear and grapefruit and twitched myself into a semblance of sleep.

The weather seemed to be following a pattern. There would be a strong wind during the day, squalls in the afternoon, and then, in the evening, the winds and the sea would die down somewhat. Each day the waves were higher and stronger. I knew why: the wind was rubbing the surface of the Gulf

Stream the wrong way, and even at this distance we were feeling the effects.

One night the winds did not lessen in intensity. Instead they built up to gale force. Soon they were accompanied by torrents of rain and almost continuous lightning.

I was facing my first storm at sea. For a moment I thought back to the near-tornado *Yankee Girl* and I had weathered on White Bear Lake; I was glad I'd had that experience. Now I would put it to use.

Yankee Girl's mast was grounded, but a stray spark passing through the cabin could still ignite the gas I kept smelling whenever the hatch was closed. I wasn't sure whether the containers were releasing actual fumes into the air, but the odor was enough to make me nervous. I didn't like sitting and sleeping on top of all that gasoline.

Gradually the lightning faded and the wind died down to a whisper.

"That wasn't so bad, was it?" my friend wanted to know.

"Not bad at all," I agreed.

Day after day the squalls became more frequent. They popped over the horizon regularly, driving the rains before them like steel-gray curtains. While before they had come singly or from one direction, they now burst forth in groups of from six to eight at a time, marching across the sea in lines I couldn't avoid.

Each time I saw one approaching, I rushed to drop and lash the sails. Then I braced myself for the 60 knot winds and sheets of lightning I was sure would follow. Again and again I crouched in the cabin with the hatch tightly secured, waiting for something terrible to happen. But nothing ever did. The squalls always passed over, bringing only light winds and misty rain.

After a few days I realized that these offshore squalls were very different from the ones I'd encountered along the coast. From that point on I just sailed right through them without even bothering to douse my sails.

Once, as the latest group of squalls cleared, a rainbow appeared in the distance off my port bow. Startled, I pushed back my cap and stared at it.

I had seen innumerable rainbows over inland lakes and fields, but I had never even imagined one at sea. It arced perfectly over the churning waters, its colors brilliant and clear.

This incredible beauty was a gift I hadn't expected. As I sat at the tiller, bobbing up and down with the motion of the waves and looking up at the sky, I wondered how I had come to be favored with such a sight. Was the rainbow meant as a message, a sign to me that I wasn't really alone? Suddenly I was overcome by a profound sense of peace and joy, as if a hand had reached out to touch me when I most needed it.

The mood stayed with me long after the rainbow had faded and the skies had taken on their familiar shade of gray. Out here by myself, I was beginning to appreciate the vast disparity between my little world and the immensity of God's creation. Hour after hour, I was feeling closer to God then I'd ever felt before.

"You know," my friend said, "God must be a great guy. Who else would take the time to make a rainbow—and why?"

Something peculiar was happening. Whenever I pointed *Yankee Girl* toward our east-southeast heading, she buried her bow in a wall of water.

The wind was shifting again.

Now I had another difficult decision to make. Should I head south, or north? Any attempt to keep going east would be fruitless.

I could hope that the wind would continue to change and come around to my starboard beam, but that might take a long time. At this point I was being pushed to the south. When I came over on the starboard tack and tried to force

Yankee Girl to the northeast, the wind and the waves drove me due north.

"First it was Africa, and now it's Nova Scotia," my friend said gleefully. "Where are we going?"

I battled the wind in silence.

"Of course we could always stop in Halifax, rest up, and start over again," he continued.

"Let's hope not," I said.

My friend's suggestion was a distinct possibility, though. After four days at sea, I had not yet reached the Gulf Stream. I was cold, tired, miserable, and unsure of my position. I'd averaged, at best, only 35 miles a day since my journey began. At that rate it would take me 100 days to make the crossing.

"You're going to eat a little light for those last ten days, aren't you?" my friend asked, needling me.

"Even toothpaste has a few calories," I shot back.

I reflected on my predicament. These were unusual and almost freakish weather conditions for this time of year; I wasn't supposed to be bucking easterly winds. I had left on June 1 for the specific purpose of encountering favorable winds, and I felt cheated.

Two and a half years of reading, research, planning, and preparation—and here I was, with the possibility of failure hanging over me like a shadow.

It seemed obvious that I would have to stop and perhaps even turn back. Instead I gritted my teeth and reverted to my southeasterly direction. I would keep fighting for as long as I could.

"Better Bermuda than Nova Scotia," my friend consoled me.

"At least it's warm there," I admitted.

The fifth day dawned bright and clear. Even though I was motoring right into its glare, I was glad to see the sun again. The wind was down, and for the first time I could see the full horizon without having my view interrupted by waves.

"If only you'd thought to bring along 90 more gallons of

gas," my friend chimed in. "You'd have it made."

"You're starting to get on my nerves," I told him. "Don't forget—you're supposed to cheer me up."

At about 11:30 A.M. the wind had died down completely. The surface of the water was as flat as a billiard table and almost as green.

This was the moment I had been waiting for. Eagerly I shut down the outboard, dove into the cabin, and grabbed my bottle of Joy dishwashing detergent. Then, after stripping off my long-sleeved shirt and flinging my cap below, I leaned over the port side as far as I could.

Yankee Girl responded by heeling over about a foot under my weight—enough for me to dip my hands into the ocean and splash water over my head.

It was enjoying my first shampoo in five days.

I had to wash and rinse my hair three times to remove the accumulated salt and sweat, but the cool wetness felt good. I tried not to think about what I might bring up in my next handful of sea water: a Portuguese man-of-war on my arm or head would be no joke.

I was reaching into the Atlantic, my eyes screwed shut to keep out the salt and soapsuds, when a loud *whoo-oo-oo-sh* made me jerk upright. With my eyes burning and lather running down my face, I stared at the water in front of my boat, transfixed.

From no more than 15 feet away, a pilot whale was looking directly at me. We locked eyes for what seemed like ages. Then, with a twist of his great dark body, he slid beneath the waves.

Suddenly I realized that he was not alone. He was leading about a dozen other whales, some of them cows with calves at their sides. They glided toward me and lazily circled *Yankee Girl*, perhaps wondering what this blue-and-green toy was doing on their ocean. Finally, their curiosity satisfied, they slowly swam off to the north.

These were not the first whales I'd encountered since leaving

Chesapeake Bay. Only the day before, at about dusk, I'd noticed a large black shape in the water ahead. As I drew closer, it appeared to be sleeping, its long body rising and falling rhythmically and its dorsal fin sticking up above the surface. When it became apparent that it wasn't going to charge me, I put the tiller hard over and passed about 50 yards behind it. Only then did it turn and glance in my direction.

I expected to see whales throughout my crossing, but I hoped that they'd leave me alone. Whales can be very aggressive and unpredictable. They've been known to sink sailboats and, in the old days of whaling, even ships. With luck, the ones I met in the future would be as benign as those whose paths I'd crossed so far.

I watched the pilot whales until they disappeared from view. They *were* beautiful—especially when they were swimming away from me and my tiny boat.

I motored along through the afternoon. At about 3:00 P.M., while I was peering out into the distance, I saw something that nearly took my breath away. With growing excitement, I grabbed for my binoculars and focused on what looked like a tiny white triangle shimmering on the horizon.

It was a sail!

The prospect of meeting another boat cheered me enormously. The mere sight of a human face would help to counteract the feelings of depression that had been weighing heavily on me during the past few days. I wasn't about to give up—not yet—but the frustration, loneliness, and contrary winds had taken their toll. What a boost it would be if I could have someone to talk to, if only for a little while!

I turned up my Evinrude another few hundred rpm's in anticipation.

"Maybe he can give us a position," my imaginary friend suggested. "Or maybe he has a single-side band and we can radio a message home."

But the sailboat maintained its pace and distance. In truth, my chances of overtaking it were remote.

At about 3:30 P.M. the sun was low enough for me to take a sight for longitude. I was very uncertain of my position at that point in time; I could only guess at the distance I'd covered, and I had no idea where the currents had carried me. So, after carefully unshipping my primary sextant, I took a shot.

As I began converting the signs to a fix, I experienced a wave of seasickness. I made a few calculations and lay down to rest. Then I made a few more and rested again, fighting my nausea. At this rate it would take me more than 30 minutes to do what I'd normally be able to accomplish in five.

My position, as it turned out, wasn't all that encouraging. The fix I got—37 degrees 5 minutes N, 72 degrees 25 minutes W—revealed that *Yankee Girl* and I had made only 160 nautical miles since our departure. That meant that we'd been averaging 32 miles a day. At that rate it really *would* take 100 days for us to make the crossing.

But at least I now knew where we were. All I could do was hope that the Gulf Stream wasn't too far ahead.

I had originally thought that I'd catch the current somewhere between 75 and 90 miles out of the bay; that's where the people in Virginia Beach told me it would be. In retrospect, I realized that they probably hadn't been out that far themselves and didn't actually know. I should have checked these figures more carefully myself, but at the time it didn't seem that important. I figured that I would just keep sailing until I got there. But instead of arriving at the Gulf Stream within two days, I was already in the middle of my fifth day at sea and still hadn't found it.

The error in my planning didn't bother me that much. What did disturb me was the fact that by neglecting this one detail I'd set myself up for a major disappointment. I was depressed due to my failure to reach the Gulf Stream on schedule, and depression can be dangerous for a singlehander.

Acknowledging my mistake made me feel a little better.

By about 5 P.M. I was close enough to the other boat to see that she was a sloop. But then, when I was starting to believe that I might close on her soon, she veered off sharply to the southeast. Maybe her crew had decided to head for Bermuda; I didn't know. I just knew that I suddenly felt more alone and discouraged than ever.

As night wore on, a magnificent breeze came up, and that lifted my spirits. I raised my twin jibs and soon *Yankee Girl* was ghosting along at a couple of knots. When the stars started appearing in the sky, I hoisted my strobe light to the masthead. The brilliant light reflected off the sails like a beacon. I told myself that a passing ship couldn't help but see me.

Up until this point of my journey I had eaten no hot meals. Considering the condition of the sea, the weather, and my stomach, it seemed like a good time to try. Amazingly, I even felt a bit hungry. For five days I had subsisted on apples, oranges, jerky, crackers, granola bars, and an occasional peanut butter and jelly sandwich. But tonight, I decided, I would feast on one of my favorite sailing foods: Dinty Moore beef stew.

Because of the gasoline smell in the cabin, I was afraid to light the stove there. So I held it on the cabin top while I heated my one-course dinner.

"Now *this* is living," I told my friend. "Hot stew, a beautiful night, and a boat steering herself for England."

"How about some music?" my friend asked.

"Good idea," I answered, reaching for the tape recorder. "Will Linda Ronstadt do?"

We listened to *Blue Bayou* over and over again as the miles slid away behind us.

I spent the next two days motoring. When there was a wind, it was against me. In periods of calm I held my umbrella up to protect myself from the sun.

At least I was over my initial motion sickness. From here on

I'd be fine no matter how rough it got.

After having been at the tiller for the whole sixth day, I was exhausted when darkness fell. More determined than before to reach the Gulf Stream, I kept on going long into the night, steering by the stars. When I finally gave up at about 10 P.M., I slumped down on my abbreviated bunk without ceremony. That night I didn't even notice the grapefruit.

I had more problems the following afternoon. I had been motor-sailing all morning long, but then the wind, which usually came up out of the northeast during that time of day, swung directly out of the east. I had to quit. There wasn't much sense in wasting precious fuel beating into those head seas.

Under these conditions the best I could do was to slow my drift back toward Virginia. I dug down under my sleeping bag and clothing and pulled out my sea anchor, a six-foot-long heavy nylon drogue.

The cone-shaped anchor had been designed to hold a boat of up to 25 feet in length. I had experimented with it on White Bear Lake, but I had never used it in waves this high or with *Yankee Girl*'s new rudder. I still had hopes that it would either put a stop to my drift or temper the constant rolling of the boat.

But *Yankee Girl* had other ideas. As soon as I attached the anchor to 200 feet of ⅜-inch nylon line and streamed it from her bow, she was up to her old tricks. She sailed right past it, turned downwind, and, like a puppy pulling a blanket, dragged it along behind her.

"All right," I said aloud, "if that's the way you want to be, we'll try it from the stern." That, I thought, would at least allow her to lie comfortably.

When I moved the anchor, the waves began breaking hard against *Yankee Girl*'s transom. If the weather worsened, I knew, they would wash right into the cabin.

Sighing, I retrieved the anchor and put it back into its plastic bag. I considered throwing it away, but then it occurred to me that it might be useful at some point in the future. For what, I didn't know, because it was clear that *Yankee Girl* wasn't going to lie to it. At any rate, I elected to keep it.

It wasn't long before I regretted that decision. Somehow the sea anchor's bag had become torn, and it wasn't long before I found myself sitting in a small pool of salt water.

I didn't really mind having to change my pants and underwear, for it had been days since I'd put on clean clothing. But it was hard work in these cramped conditions.

First I had to climb forward into the bow, which meant moving a lot of gear aft. Then I had to untie the sail bags and dig through them until I found the right one-gallon plastic containers. After wriggling my way back to the stern, I had to figure out how to remove my clammy clothing in a space which allowed me neither to sit up nor stretch out. The whole process took nearly half an hour.

Meanwhile the rolling and pitching motion was getting on my nerves. It seemed like the only way to escape it was to heave to. Clambering onto the cabin top, I hoisted the sails.

With the main sheeted in tight, the jib brought across to the windward side, and the tiller hard alee, *Yankee Girl* was, for all practical purposes, "parked." She could head up and fall off, but she couldn't go anywhere.

We weren't moving forward, but we weren't moving backward either. And at least the up-and-down motion was dampened somewhat by the pressure of the wind on the sails.

I slid the hatch closed. Once more I was secure inside my tiny tossing cabin. Though I felt physically safe, the isolation and fatigue were wearing me down. I had spoken to no one for an entire week, and I was beginning to worry about Sally, my family, and my friends.

I'd thought that I'd be able to speak with an occasional ship and have its radio operator send a message back to the Coast Guard. I knew that Sally would be checking with them frequently; word from me would ease her mind tremendously. But although I'd tried to reach half a dozen passing ships on my VHF radio-telephone, I'd never received a reply.

Once a ship had passed by very close—within a quarter of a mile—and I had steered in her direction. During the whole time I'd kept repeating "WXQ 9864 . . . this is the yacht *Yankee Girl* calling any ship in the area." Nothing had ever come back, and I'd wondered if my radio was working. Although I'd radioed my message over and over, the ship had simply sailed away.

Did this mean that part of my backup plan was useless? That I wouldn't be able to count on help from other ships if I became ill or *Yankee Girl* was badly damaged? I wouldn't know until I tried again.

It was already the evening of my seventh day out, and nothing had gone the way I'd planned. I'd been averaging only 32 miles a day. I had been forced to motor nearly all of that distance and had used up one-third of my gasoline supply. The wind and the waves seemed determined to push me backward. And the Gulf Stream was nowhere in sight.

If conditions didn't improve, my food and water would run out long before I reached England.

"Cheer up," my friend said. "Things can't get much worse."

Silently I wondered how long it would be before they got better.

VII

The Gathering Easterly

"He that will learn to pray,
let him go to sea."
George Herbert

Again and again *Yankee Girl* and I were lifted up 10 or 12 feet, held there for an instant, and dropped with a sickening lurch. Meanwhile we were tossed sideways, first in one direction and then the other.

For two solid days the Atlantic had been a gigantic rollercoaster. We were hove to, stopped by an easterly wind that had gradually increased to gales of 30 knots. I was taking a beating from the mountainous waves that often broke right over the boat, but *Yankee Girl* seemed to be in her element. With nothing up but her reefed mainsail, she stayed heeled over at about 30 degrees. She'd move forward a bit, retreat when she was hit by a wall of water, heel some more, and stubbornly resume her northeasterly heading.

Every time she raced down the face of a wave, I hung on for dear life. Then I waited for the bone-jarring *snap* which meant that she'd buried her bow in another massive wave.

I had no way of knowing where we were. Perhaps we were being driven even further away from the elusive Gulf Stream.

Although I had counted on reaching the Stream within twenty-four hours after leaving Virginia, I had been at sea for eight miserable days now and had not yet found it. The water temperature had been rising steadily—from 63 degrees off Norfolk to a present reading of 74 degrees—but that was still not warm enough; the normal temperature of the Stream was 81 degrees.

I kept leaning over the side of the boat, hoping to see the violet-blue color and decreased phosphorescence that are the Stream's physical characteristics. But I was always disappointed. The water remained a leaden green.

All told, I had seen the sun only three times since I'd begun my crossing and had had no more than 12 hours of favorable winds. I was feeling cheated—not by myself or by *Yankee Girl*, but by the freak wind that was holding me back when I should have been speeding toward England.

To make matters worse, I had gotten no real sleep in days. Inside the cramped cabin, the air was hot and stuffy. I couldn't open the ventilator because the waves breaking over the boat invariably surged in. Whenever I tried to leave the hatch open a crack, I was drenched. I had to content myself with an occasional gulp of fresh air and a faceful of stinging spray.

Toward the dawn of the ninth day, bruised and fatigued, I finally crawled up into the bow as far as I could go and wedged myself in among the grapefruit and gear. The tiny pocket of air around me quickly became stale with the combination of my breathing and the smell of gasoline. For once I didn't care. At least I could lie there without being slammed around.

As I listened to the pounding of the waves on *Yankee Girl*'s hull, I went over my calculations again.

England was still more than 3,000 miles away.

I was averaging about 32 miles per day.

At this rate it would take me more than 100 days to reach my destination.

I had a 90-day supply of food and water on board.

"We'll make it," my imaginary friend said encouragingly. "We just have to keep our spirits up."

That was proving to be the most difficult task of all. I had spent a whole year prior to my voyage preparing myself physically and psychologically for whatever the sea might offer, but I had never dreamed that I'd encounter such adverse conditions so soon.

On the morning of my departure, I'd almost felt capable of *walking* across the Atlantic—I was that sure of myself and my plan. Since then I'd been fighting a growing depression. Frustrated and weary, I wondered how much more I could take before I'd have to turn back.

By late afternoon of the ninth day there was a gnawing in my stomach. This was a warning to me that I needed to eat something solid. I groped forward and found an orange. It wasn't much, but I knew that my stomach could tolerate it. Maybe later I'd make myself a sandwich.

As I chewed on the last section of the orange, I reached out over the drop board in the transom to rinse my hands in the sea.

The water was as warm as a bath.

Holding my breath, I checked it with the thermometer: 81 degrees.

The Gulf Stream. At last.

The next day the wind continued to head us, blowing directly out of the east. I was having trouble controlling my impatience.

"It can't last forever," my friend said.

"Can't it?" I answered testily. I was in no mood for a conversation. Now that I had reached the Gulf Stream, I wanted to get going.

In the morning, just before sunrise, the wind died. With my hopes rising, I dropped the slatting main and lay down for some badly needed rest. But I had no sooner curled myself on my bunk than the wind came up from the east as hard as before.

Later, when I checked the water temperature, I was shocked to discover that it had dropped to 78 degrees.

The treacherous easterly had pushed us back out of the Gulf Stream.

Desperately I hoisted the main and tried to sail southeast. *Yankee Girl* leaped from crest to crest, burying her bow in each oncoming wave and then coming up for air.

Once again we were sailing a zigzag course for nowhere.

I glanced at my hand on the tiller. After more than a week of exposure to wind and water, it was begining to look like a huge white prune. As I examined it more closely, I noticed something else. The constant wetness had softened the skin and caused old scars to reappear. Fascinated, I studied each one as if it had been a photograph in a family album. All of my past mistakes and scrapes came back to haunt me.

That made me wonder what my face must look like. I was sure that my eyes were bloodshot and my cheeks white and pasty beneath my dark stubble of beard. Although I had three mirrors on board, I knew better than to reach for one. I had done that years earlier, during a voyage I'd made off the coast of Nicaragua, and it had been a mistake. Some things are better left unseen.

"Don't worry," my friend interjected. "You probably don't look as bad as you think you do."

I would have to take stock of my appearance at some point. If I did meet another boat, I didn't want to scare its crew to death.

As I sat huddled inside the tightly closed cabin, the waves

grew steeper and broke more frequently. At times the sea completely covered us, and I found myself staring out the portholes into green water. Wryly, I remembered the people I'd met who'd mistakenly labeled my boat a submarine. She certainly seemed to have the potential.

By early afternoon I realized that I couldn't subject *Yankee Girl* to this beating any longer. Reluctantly, I hove to. Then, out of curiosity, I checked the water temperature.

The thermometer read 81 degrees.

We were in the Gulf Stream again.

It seemed as if we were caught in the middle of a giant tug-of-war between the elements. The wind wanted to drive us one way while the current wanted to carry us another. If only they'd work together!

Lying on my side in my cramped quarters, I thought about some of the people who claimed to have "conquered" the seas, or the air, or the mountains, or the desert—or anything else in our world. To me, that was just talk. Human beings never "conquered" anything in nature; sometimes they were able to accomplish tremendous feats, but that was usually when nature was looking the other way.

I was startled out of my reverie by a loud *bla-a-a-a-a-at*.

I jumped up and threw open the hatch.

A fishing trawler was heading toward me, rolling and pitching through the waves. The noise I'd heard had been her horn sounding.

Frantically I waved my arms over my head. Hundreds of thoughts raced through my mind. After these many days of isolation, I wanted desperately to talk to someone—anyone. I wanted to get a message through to Sally and my parents. I wanted to confirm my position.

But most of all I wanted to communicate with other human beings.

Three burly fishermen, dressed in gray, grinned and waved back.

Diving below, I turned on my radio.

"This is the yacht *Yankee Girl* calling any ship in the area. This is the yacht *Yankee Girl* calling any ship in the area."

Then I eagerly awaited their response.

There was none.

I repeated my call. Again, nothing.

I heaved myself up through the hatch, waved some more, and elaborately pantomimed the act of talking and listening on a radio, pointing first at myself and then at the amused fishermen. By this time their boat had slowed down and was about 150 feet away from me, heading across my bow. From this distance I could make out the name on her transom and determine that her home port was Buenos Aires.

Obviously entertained by my antics, the crew continued to smile and wave as they left me in their wake. I went below again and repeated my call, hoping against hope that they would answer, but they never did.

Maybe they didn't understand English. Maybe they had their radio turned to another frequency. Or maybe they just didn't feel like talking. At any rate, it was clear that I wasn't going to have the conversation I longed for.

I almost wished I hadn't seen them at all.

I stood in the open hatch and stared at the trawler until she dissolved into a smudge on the horizon.

As the sky darkened, I wearily reconciled myself to another night of solitude. The appearance of the fishing boat—and my inability to reach its crew—had only increased my sense of loneliness, my feeling of being cut off from everything and everyone I valued.

I rummaged about in the forepeak, guided only by the tiny light from my radio dial. Eventually I found what I was looking for: the plastic jug that contained my clean T-shirts. Hurriedly I unscrewed the cap, brought the jug up to my face, and inhaled deeply.

I no longer heard the *whoosh* of my little boat moving through the water, the whine of the wind in the rigging, or the multitude of sounds made by gear shifting inside the hull. I no longer felt the bow shuddering against the waves or the rattle of the shrouds.

I don't know for how many minutes I sat there, hunched over a plastic container and simply breathing in the scents of freshly washed clothing and crisp Minnesota air.

I had escaped. I was home!

When I awoke the next morning, I lay for a few moments on my cramped bunk feeling sorry for myself. As usual, the cabin was chilly and damp, and my muscles ached worse than ever.

It was the beginning of my tenth day at sea, and I was bored and restless. Maybe today the imprisoning easterly winds would finally swing around and release us. Something *had* to happen soon.

In fact, the wind was shifting to the southeast, slowly but surely. Yawning, I slid the hatch open and surveyed the grey swells. The seas were still steep-sided, and *Yankee Girl*'s bow still pounded into the waves. Hove to, she made no progress, but she rose bravely to meet each new wave as if she could bluff her way to England.

I had to at least *try* to do some sailing today. I couldn't stand the thought of staying in the same spot for another 24 hours.

With the wind moving around to the southeast, I felt as if I might have a chance. I released the lines securing the tiller, brought the rudder over, and fell off on the starboard tack.

Yankee Girl veered north and then northeast, climbing the waves one by one. Although it seemed as if we were moving through the water, I knew that this was only an illusion. Our forward motion was negligible.

I felt like a hamster in a cage—running around and around a wheel and getting nowhere.

"Might as well heave to again, Ger," my friend suggested.

"If you say so," I replied, gladly putting the tiller hard over.

It was clear that another day of misery lay ahead. I would just have to concentrate on being patient and reestablishing my positive attitude.

"You'll be laughing about this soon," my friend said cheerfully. "Once the wind shifts, you'll be flying."

"I hope you're right," I answered.

By now I was so tired of fighting the constant lurching of the boat that all I could do was lie on my bunk and hang on. At least that would keep me from accumulating any more bruises.

Every hour or so throughout the day I clambered back to the inspection port in the drop board and peered out over the Atlantic. And each time the same scene greeted me: endless miles of tossing water beneath a pale sky.

Once I was just about to lie back down when I glanced out a porthole and saw a larger-than-ordinary patch of white.

Rogue wave, I thought immediately. A wave of that type, caused by two or more waves suddenly combining forces, could crash down on top of *Yankee Girl* in a dangerous flurry of foam.

I waited until we reached the crest of the next wave. Then I saw the patch of white again—and gasped.

It was a ship!

I felt the blood pounding in my temples. The mere fact that I had seen her was a miracle. Normally I wouldn't have bothered to look out a porthole when the sea was this rough; the waves blocked my view. But somehow I had managed to turn my head at just the right time. If I hadn't, I may not have seen her—and she would almost certainly have passed by without seeing me.

I jumped to my radio.

"WXQ 9864 . . . WXQ 9864 . . . This is the yacht *Yankee Girl* calling any ship in the area . . . Over." I was almost yelling into the mike.

Age 4

Yankee Doodle in 1969 prior to my first major voyage—down the Mississippi from St. Paul, Minnesota, through the Caribbean to Panama, and finally to South America

My father, Louis, sailed with me on *Yankee Doodle* from Iowa to St. Louis

Yankee Spirit on White Bear Lake in 1974; I had planned
to take her around the world but barely made it back to Miami
after only 53 hours at sea

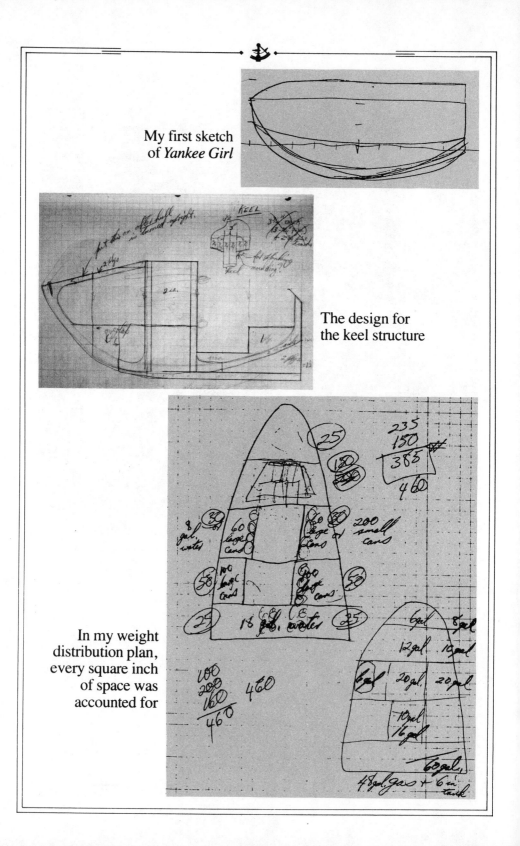

My first sketch
of *Yankee Girl*

The design for
the keel structure

In my weight
distribution plan,
every square inch
of space was
accounted for

My original sail plan
called for *Yankee Girl*
to carry a little more
than 80 square feet
of working sail

I often worked at
my drawing board
late into the night

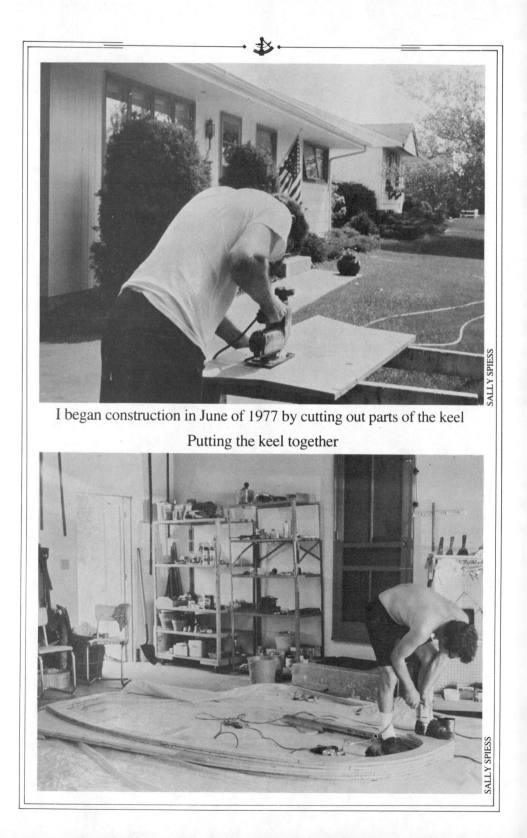

I began construction in June of 1977 by cutting out parts of the keel

Putting the keel together

With the frame completed and the bottom planking attached, I was
ready to start working on the side planking

Once the side planking was on, I draped 10-oz. fiberglass cloth over the hull prior to saturating it with polyester resin

Soaked with resin, the fiberglass cloth became transparent and hugged the boat like a skin

GERRY SPIESS

GERRY SPIESS

With the hull
planed and
glassed, I could
begin working
on the interior
of the boat—
building the
lockers and
bunk and
painting them

GERRY SPIESS

The framework
for the cabin top
and deck

GERRY SPIESS

Glassing the
cabin; soon the
whole boat
would be
sheathed in
fiberglass cloth

SALLY SPIESS

In September, 1977, after three months of construction and several coats of paint, my little boat was finally ready to be launched

SALLY SPIESS

Tally's Anchor Inn, where *Yankee Girl* was moored

On White Bear Lake
in the fall of 1977

Practicing using
my sextant

My mother, Jeanette, did her best to talk me out of my plans for an Atlantic crossing

During the summer of 1978, I often spent the night on board *Yankee Girl*

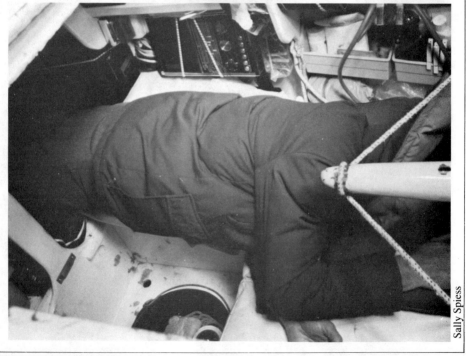

The day before I left for Virginia, Sally and I posed for a final picture in front of *Yankee Girl*

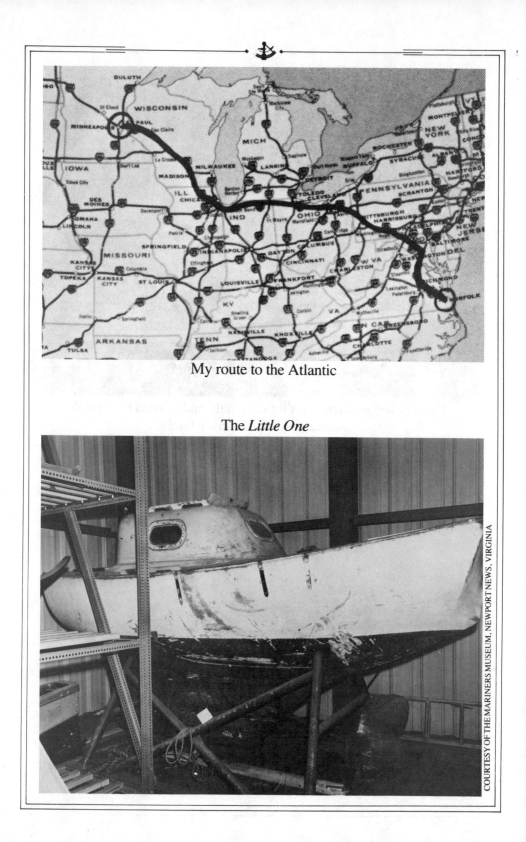

My route to the Atlantic

The *Little One*

Yankee Girl in her slip at Lynnhaven Municipal Marina

GERRY SPIESS

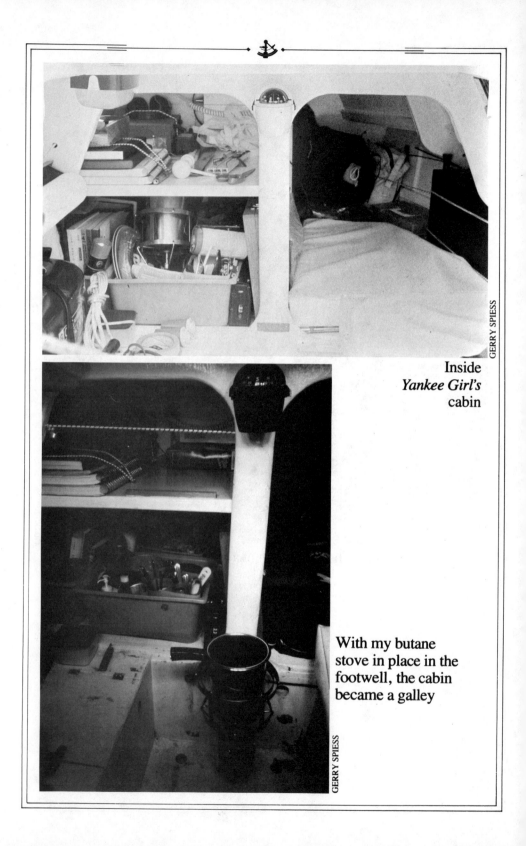

GERRY SPIESS

Inside
Yankee Girl's
cabin

With my butane
stove in place in the
footwell, the cabin
became a galley

GERRY SPIESS

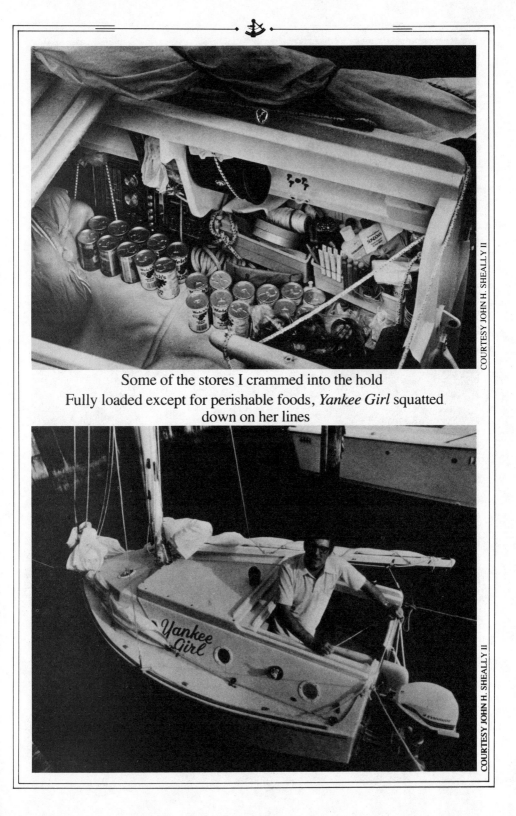

Some of the stores I crammed into the hold

Fully loaded except for perishable foods, *Yankee Girl* squatted
down on her lines

GERRY SPIESS

I taped this picture of Sally inside the cover of my navigation box

I attached these two plaques to the inside of the cabin; they would buoy my spirits in the lonely days ahead

With Sam Murphey the night before my departure

June 1, 1979

As I sailed out of Chesapeake Bay, I put on my safety harness—
which I would wear throughout the crossing

Ahead: the North Atlantic

GERRY SPIESS

GERRY SPIESS

At sea

The Atlantic in a rare benign mood

One of the many oil drums
I saw during my crossing

These ships, like many others,
passed me by without responding
to my call

The rocky coast of Cornwall

Aboard the *Link*, Sally and Jason Davis spotted
Yankee Girl on the horizon

LOUIS SPIESS

I was astonished to see the *Link*—
with Sally and my parents on board

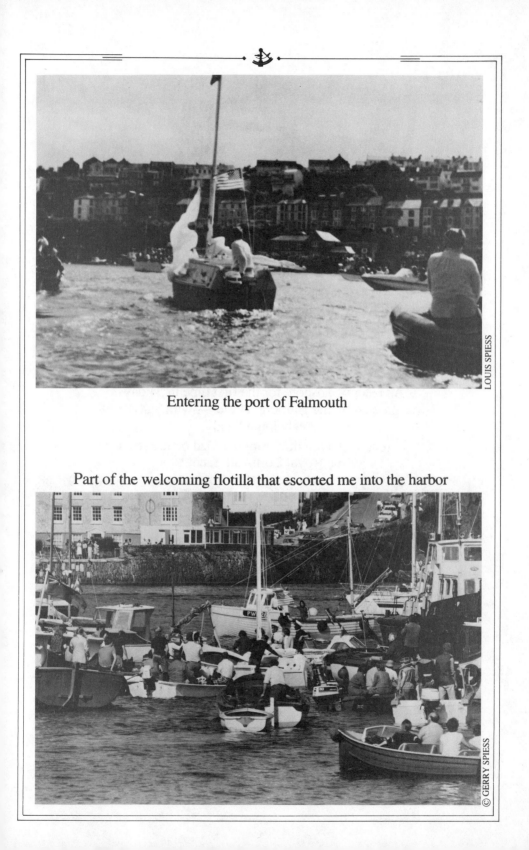

Entering the port of Falmouth

Part of the welcoming flotilla that escorted me into the harbor

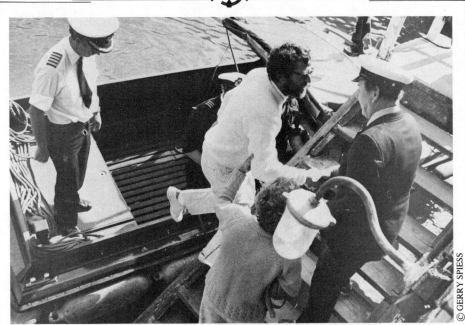

As I stepped ashore for the first time in 54 days,
I was greeted by the Harbour Master—with Sally lending
a helping hand
I received a big hug from my Dad on the steps
of the Royal Cornwall Yacht Club

A crowd surrounded Sally and me as we made our way
through the streets of Falmouth

An English journalist conducted an on-the-spot interview

The Greenbank Hotel

The official photograph of Falmouth Mayor Olive White, who greeted me warmly and graciously

With Sally at the Greenbank Hotel

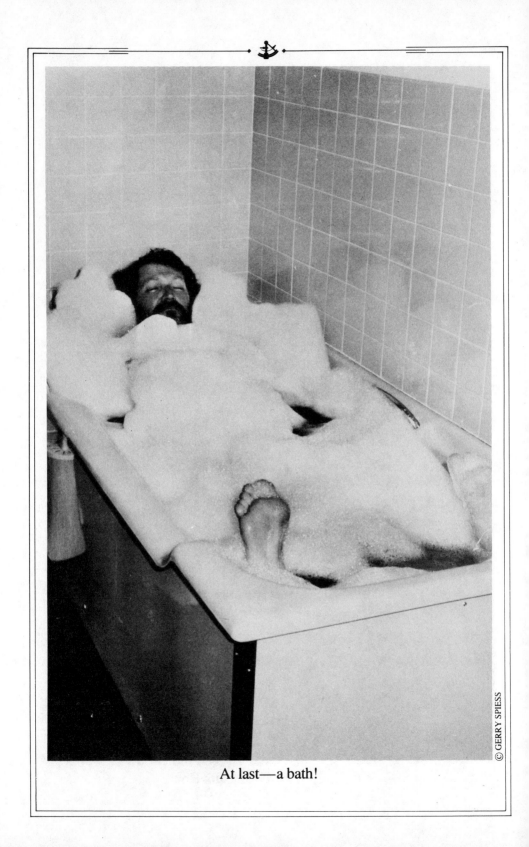

At last—a bath!

Biting my lip and holding my breath, I waited. I was about to repeat my call when a voice with a Dutch accent came back over the airwaves.

"Is that the very little sailboat?" it asked.

"YES!" I shouted. "And it's *wonderful* to talk to someone!"

I was on the verge of tears. After 11 days of not hearing another human voice, I found it difficult to talk. I had to turn away from the mike for a moment; my emotions were too overpowering.

Finally I managed to calm myself down.

"You will never know how much I appreciate your being on Channel 16," I said. "I've called other ships during the past week, but none of them have responded."

"We always monitor 16," the voice answered crisply. "All good ships do."

I breathed deeply. This was clearly a professional crew.

I soon learned that I was talking with the Dutch container ship *Bilderdyk* out of Amsterdam.

"Can you give me a position check?" I inquired.

"Certainly. Please stand by."

There was a pause.

"You are at 38 degrees 8 minutes north latitude, 64 degrees 55 minutes west longitude."

I was elated. My position wasn't that far off from what I had estimated.

"Thank you," I said. "Would you mind relaying a message back to the States for me?"

"Not at all."

I gave them my message and we chatted for a few minutes more. Then, as I watched from my porthole, they were gone— on their way again, hidden by the waves.

Now I did start to cry; I couldn't help it. After so many days of complete isolation, my simple conversation with the Dutch ship had put me back in touch with the world. With their leaving, I was alone again—alone with my aching fatigue, solitude, discomfort, and fear.

I relived that brief encounter many times throughout the night.

Gerry would love these flowers, Sally thought to herself as she walked to the kitchen sink with an armful of Peace roses.

They had just begun to bloom, and this was the first cutting. Their sweet scent filled the room.

Sally glanced at the large wooden wall clock Gerry had built. It was nearly 9 P.M. She had been working in the garden for almost an hour.

It was a beautiful summer evening. The air was full of the clean fragrance of freshly cut grass, and a soft breeze blew off of nearby White Bear Lake.

When the telephone rang, Sally carefully lay the roses on the countertop before moving to answer it.

Maybe it was Jeanette, Gerry's mother. Or maybe it was Bill Mezzano calling to see if she needed anything.

"Hello?" she said.

It was then that she heard the unmistakeable crackle of long distance coming over the wire.

"Mrs. Spiess?" a clipped voice asked. "This is the officer on watch at the U.S. Coast Guard Station at Portsmouth, Virginia."

Sally inhaled sharply. Why would the Coast Guard be calling? Had something gone wrong?

"The Dutch ship *Bilderdyk* has reported contact with *Yankee Girl*," the voice continued. "Your husband's position is 38 degrees 8 minutes north latitude, 64 degrees 55 minutes west longitude."

"Just a minute!" Sally said as she shakily reached for a pencil and a notepad. "Please repeat his position."

The Coast Guard officer slowly gave her the figures again.

"He also sent along a message for you: 'Everything is okay.' Got that?" he inquired politely.

"Yes, thanks," Sally replied as she hung up.

For a moment she just stared at the numbers on the notepad. Then she ran to the den.

On the wall was a map of the North Atlantic. When Sally had finished plotting Gerry's position, she stepped back and studied the map.

Gerry was only 500 miles out. Why hadn't he made more progress? Had he been becalmed?

She looked down at the message she had written. *Everything is OK.* She read it again and again.

Sally stood in front of the map for a long time, holding the pad in her hand. Somehow the numbers and words formed a connection between her and her husband, a thin thread stretching over thousands of miles that bound them together.

Then she walked back into the kitchen to call Gerry's mother and father.

On the following day the Associated Press carried a report on its wire services which it had received from the Coast Guard. It read:

> Gerry Spiess has messaged home that "all is well" in his record-breaking attempt to sail across the Atlantic in a 10-foot boat, the Coast Guard said. Spiess, 39, of White Bear Lake, Minn., made radio contact with a Dutch cargo ship Monday while about 500 miles off Virginia Beach, from which he departed June 1 for a 3,000-mile voyage to Falmouth, England, officials said.

> "He is chugging right along," said Coast Guard spokesman Fred Maldonado. "He sent us a message to tell his family things are fine."

VIII

Storm Over the North Atlantic

"Woe to him that is alone
when he falleth; for he hath
not another to help him up."
Ecclesiastes 4:10

After four days of gradually worsening weather, the Atlantic had finally erupted into violence. Long lines of waves advanced out of the south and the east simultaneously; when they met, they crested and broke in towers of roaring, churning foam. The peaks were larger than any I had ever seen—some were as tall as *Yankee Girl*'s mast.

Braced inside the cabin, I was at the mercy of the sea. There was nothing I could do against the shifting, blinding walls of water that surrounded us. They came with the sound of freight trains and broke over the boat like thunder. Again and again *Yankee Girl* reeled as if she had been hit with a giant sledgehammer.

It was the fourteenth day of my voyage and the third day of the storm. Three days of booming waves and shrieking winds, of never-ending motion and aching fatigue.

When the wind had begun to shift from its easterly position, I had hoped that it would continue to veer around to the west. Instead it had swung to the south and was now blowing across the Gulf Stream at speeds of over 40 knots. The changing wind and the Stream's current were locked in a deadly battle. The Stream wanted to flow one way; the gale wanted to push another.

The resulting crosswaves, some of which were 15 feet tall, were coming about eight to ten seconds apart. I had to listen for them, for I could see nothing out my portholes. *Yankee Girl* was closed up like a coffin with me inside.

Her movement through the water was frighteningly erratic. Rather than climbing up the face of each wave and then surging down its back into the trough, she rose and fell with a *whump*, then rose abruptly and fell again.

When the storm began, I had tried strapping myself down with my seat belt. But while that had held my trunk secure, my arms and legs had flopped up and down and my head had been jerked from side to side. Finally I had crawled up into the bow, turned sideways, and wedged my knees against the navigation box and my head between my first-aid kit and a sail bag. This dampened my side-to-side motion, but I still had to brace my arm against the ceiling to keep from being slammed up and down.

I was in constant pain. In the beginning I had been able to open the hatch, kneel there for a moment, and then slowly straighten my back. But now this was no longer possible. My muscles were sore beyond belief, and my hips were badly bruised.

Inside the tiny cabin the air was stuffy and hot. When I did manage to fall into an exhausted sleep, I awoke almost immediately, gasping for breath. Then I would slide the hatch back a few inches, risking a faceful of water for the fresh air I so desperately needed.

Water was leaking in around the closed hatch and through the tiller opening. The blue ripstop nylon flap fastened around the tiller where it came through the transom kept pulling loose. Whenever a wave slammed against the stern, water spurted in through the open flap and sprayed the inside of the boat like a firehose.

I tried to solve this problem by stuffing sponges into the gaps around the tiller. I also put towels around the hatch and secured it more tightly by hammering a screwdriver in on one side and jamming my ballpoint pen into the other. These emergency measures helped—a little. The water still came in, but with less force.

I was continually sponging out the inside of the cabin. I would begin by mopping water from my foul-weather gear, the seat cushions, and the cabin sides. Then I would reach as far as I could into the footwell, laboriously moving and replacing each piece of gear. When my sponge was saturated, I would stop and listen to the waves crashing around the boat. A momentary hush meant that I had a little less than ten seconds in which to unscrew the inspection port in the transom, shove the sponge out, squeeze it, yank my arm back inside, and seal up the port again. If I miscalculated—even by a split second—the next wave surged up my sleeve and soaked me to the waist.

I was using an old meat baster to bail out the bilges. I would insert it down below, pump the tube full of water, and then shoot the water into my portable head—the one-gallon plastic jug, complete with screw top, in which I relieved myself during these stormy conditions. When the jug was full of bilge water, I'd pause again to gauge the waves. Then I'd quickly pull out the screwdriver and ballpoint pen I'd wedged in around the hatch, unfasten the hatch, and slide it forward a few inches. After checking for crosswaves, I'd open it just wide enough to allow me to poke my head and shoulders out and empty the jug.

Sometimes, in the intervals between waves, I'd find myself staring at the seascape. I had never before seen anything like it. Despite my pain, my overwhelming sense of fatigue, and the knowledge that I was in great danger, I could not help but marvel at its fierce beauty.

Everywhere I looked the ocean was streaked with foam, for the gale-force winds were literally ripping the tops off of the highest waves. The clouds were so low that they seemed to be riding the surface of the water. I was in another world, a world of screaming winds and mountainous waves, a world that was totally indifferent to me. I felt its enormous power— and my utter powerlessness.

All of my careful planning had come to this: three days of being tossed about by the Atlantic like a insignificant speck. I could do nothing but wait out the storm, hoping it would end before I became exhausted beyond the point of return—or before *Yankee Girl* sustained irreparable damage.

My dream had turned into a nightmare.

Hours passed, but the storm showed no signs of abating. Meanwhile I got on with the business of staying alive—and keeping my tiny boat afloat.

As I dumped another jug of bilge water, I decided to take a few seconds and resecure the fastenings on the nylon tiller flap. Too much water was still coming in. Holding tightly to the hatch coaming with one hand, I bent over the transom and grabbed the flap.

I became so engrossed in what I was doing that I forgot to pay attention to the waves.

Suddenly there was a terrible silence.

I looked up to see a solid wall of green water towering over me. It was more than 17 feet in height—taller than my mast—and it was heading right for *Yankee Girl* and her wide-open hatch.

I ducked down into the cabin and frantically slammed the

hatch shut—just as the wave broke over the boat. There was no time to lock the hatch, so I braced myself against it and held it with every ounce of my strength.

It was wrenched out of my hands.

With incredible fury and force, the water poured in. I was knocked back against the bulkhead. Stunned, I watched as the water continued to rush in—more water than *Yankee Girl* had ever taken on. I felt as if I were in a dream, a horrible dream in which everything moved in slow motion and there was no escape.

Somehow my adrenalin took over. I scrambled up, dumping a lapful of water, and literally tore at the hatch. Under my desperate clawing, it moved an inch at a time until finally it closed, shutting off the deluge.

I shook my head to clear it. Then, groggily, I surveyed the cabin. What I saw nearly caused me to panic. There was water everywhere—from the bunk on down.

I had to get it out as quickly as I could. With every lurch and roll of the boat, more of my provisions and gear were becoming saturated. I knew that, under constant exposure to salt water, my cans of food would start to rust—along with my butane cylinders.

At first with a tin can and then with the baster, I bailed. And bailed.

It was like trying to empty the ocean with a spoon.

Several hours later, on the brink of total exhaustion, I sat down to rest. Only then did I notice that I was sopping wet. My clothes were clinging to me, pasted against my body by a combination of sweat and salt water.

Piece by piece, I began to peel them off.

I hadn't undressed in days, and I wasn't prepared for what I saw in the dim light of the cabin.

I had been immersed in water for so long that my outer layer of skin had simply dissolved. As I toweled myself off, it fell away in slimy masses.

But that wasn't the worst of it. The skin on my groin had turned a fiery red, and it itched horribly. I knew what that meant, and I dreaded it: I was in the initial stages of a fungus infection. Under the best conditions, with proper care and treatment, it took days or even weeks for this type of infection to clear up. I would carry it with me all the way to England— *if* I reached England.

I reached for my talcum powder and began dusting myself with both hands. For a moment I let go of my hold on the boat.

That was my second unforgivably careless act of the day.

The rogue wave caught us broadside. I was thrown down violently, and my head struck the side of the cabin. My shoulder broke off the towel rack, and my hip hit the gas tank hard enough to leave a dent in it.

I lay on my back with my eyes closed for a few seconds, not daring to move. When I opened them again, I found myself staring straight out the starboard ports.

I was lying on the *side* of the cabin.

We had capsized!

Instinctively I scrambled upward, trying to get my weight on *Yankee Girl's* high side. Meanwhile things kept falling toward me—my hand compass, foul-weather gear, bags of batteries, and more of the ubiquitous grapefruit.

After what seemed like ages, I was up.

The scene was one of sheer pandemonium. Gear was flying through the air, and water was pouring in through the hatch on *Yankee Girl's* submerged port side.

I threw my weight on top of the bunk and pushed.

Come on, Girl, I pleaded. *Come on. Over.*

I had to right her—now. If another wave hit while we were capsized, she might roll all the way over and we could lose the mast.

Suddenly, blessedly, *Yankee Girl* popped upright. The half-

ton of supplies below her waterline had levered her mast up
out of the water.

I didn't even have time to breathe a word of thanks. First I
had to find out whether my boat had sustained any damage
on deck. As I listened to the wave pattern, I peered out a
porthole.

Part of my gear was floating away.

I slid back the hatch and gazed out over *Yankee Girl* and
the surrounding water. The six empty gasoline cans I had
lashed to the side of the cabin were gone, literally torn away
by the force of the knockdown. So was the sea anchor. I
watched helplessly as they drifted out of reach.

There was nothing I could do to save them. Even in good
weather they would have been difficult to recover. The loss of
the sea anchor didn't bother me that much—I was almost
glad to see it go—but I did mind seeing my gasoline containers bobbing off into the distance. They had been part of my
backup flotation system, and I had counted on using them if
Yankee Girl's hull were ever damaged.

A hundred pounds of emergency flotation, gone forever.

With growing anxiety, I glanced around at the back of the
boat. Had my little Evinrude been torn off its bracket? Had I
lost that too? No—I could see it bouncing along behind the
transom. At least I still had my motor. Whether it worked,
after the beating it had taken, was a question I wasn't yet
ready to face.

I looked down at my hands. They were trembling. My
adrenaline reserves were nearly used up. I felt myself slipping
backward into the hatch and gripped the rails hard, gritting
my teeth.

I had never been so frightened in my life.

At that moment, I wanted more than anything to give up—
to get away from the agony, to escape the fear. I wanted to
close my eyes and open them again and be *somewhere else*—
back home in Minnesota, in safety and security, with my family and friends.

I bowed my head. I would cry out to God for his help.

But then, surprisingly, I found myself hesitating.

I was here of my own choosing. Would it be right to ask God to save me, to get me out of a situation I'd entered into freely?

I shook my head. God had given me all of the resources I needed to survive this storm and any other that came along. It was up to me to use them—and not to ask for more.

Instead of pleading for help, I said a prayer of thanks. I was alive, and my boat was whole. That was enough.

With my last ounce of energy, I forced myself below the pitching deck once more. Then I locked the hatch and squatted down in the wet, steamy cabin.

Night was falling. In the howling, shrieking storm, I would try to sleep.

"Hey, there's a gas station!" I shouted excitedly. "That's just what we need!"

It sat like a gleaming oasis at the side of the road. I turned the wheel of my car and slowed down.

At last, a gas station! After all those miles! I smiled in relief.

But as I pulled in beside the pumps, I sensed that there was something wrong. Something dreadfully, terribly wrong. . . .

I awoke with a start. My teeth were chattering, and I was lying in a pool of perspiration.

There *was* something wrong—with me. I was losing control of my mind.

This had been going on for most of the night. I would fall into an exhausted sleep, and my subconscious would take over—trying to lift me up and away, out of my predicament and my fear.

The gas station had been the latest in a series of escape

routes my mind had fabricated. Earlier there had been a park—green and inviting—and before that a rest stop. But each time I had begun to pull off the road, I had awakened, shivering, to find myself back in the boat. The noise, the cloying stuffiness, the constant racking motion, and the darkness—*these* were reality. Not the road, or the car, or the sun shining brightly overhead, or the trees waving in the wind.

I rubbed my face, feeling the salt and the sweat and the stubble of my beard.

Rather than helping me, my dreams were making me feel even more miserable. For I knew that there was no place to stop and rest—not here, in the middle of the Atlantic, in a storm that wouldn't end.

I was suffocating. Once again I had jammed myself into the forepeak as far as I could go, with my head wedged into a narrow "V" between bags of clothing and my legs drawn up against my chest, braced against the bulkhead. It seemed as if I had to fight for every breath.

I could hear the sounds of *Yankee Girl* rushing madly through the night. As she careened down one mountainous wave after another, the Evinrude banged against the stern and wind shrieked up the slot of the bare mast. I pressed my sleeping bag against my ears to shut out the relentless din.

I had been lying on my right arm. Now, slowly, I tried to move it—and groaned aloud. Every muscle in my body was sore, and my head ached from the insidious smell of gasoline. The fire-red splotches where my skin had been rubbed off burned and itched at the same time.

Coughing and gasping, I reached for the overhead ventilator. I was acting more out of desperation than sea sense, for even as I screwed it open water blasted through it with the force of a fire hydrant. I closed it again as quickly as I could and wiped the salt water from my face and eyes.

At least that had brought me back to my senses.

I stared at the luminous hands of my wristwatch, pale green beneath the moisture-fogged crystal. It was 3 A.M.

I had to think for a moment before I realized that it would soon be dawn. I was not looking forward to another day. Instead, I found myself hoping that night would last forever, that I could continue to hide under the blanket of darkness.

The waves kept coming, rumbling and thundering like locomotives. Suddenly one broke, slamming us sideways. It was then that I heard the noise I had been dreading.

Cr-a-a-a-a-ck!

It came from somewhere beneath me, near the stem.

Grabbing my flashlight, I crawled forward. With growing apprehension, I started pulling gear from the forepeak and shoving it behind me.

I had to get down to the keel.

Fears raced through my mind. Had *Yankee Girl* finally succumbed to the pressures of the storm? Had that last wave wounded her in some way? *Was she breaking up?*

Bracing myself against her side, I hunched forward and played the light on her glue lines. This was the point where a fracture was most likely to occur. I ran the beam down one side of her stem in the forward compartment and up the other; in her white-painted bilge, a crack would be immediately visible.

Nothing.

Was my mind playing tricks on me again?

No. I *had* heard the noise. It *had* been real.

I could feel the perspiration dripping down my forehead as I searched further. Incredibly, there were no cracks, and the forward bilge was dry.

I placed my hands on the plywood planking and felt for signs of "oil-canning"—the flexing back and forth that would indicate a weakness or fracture. But even as we plunged down another wave and my breath was jolted out of me, I could feel no movement.

I *knew* I had heard a crack, the sound of breaking wood!

There had to be a problem *somewhere;* I just hadn't found it yet. Perhaps there was a split under the keel which hadn't worked its way through to the bilge.

Without being conscious of what I was doing, I reached for my life jacket.

In all of the hours I'd spent aboard *Yankee Girl*, I hadn't thought once of donning my life jacket. But now, it appeared, it was time.

If *Yankee Girl* were seriously damaged, I'd have to survive in a swamped boat. I knew that my little girl would never sink, but my life jacket would provide an extra measure of safety.

It would give me a chance to save *Yankee Girl*—if I didn't die first of cold and exposure.

I braced my foot against the side of the cabin and my back against the dented gas tank. As the next cross-wave struck, I imagined that I felt the plywood flex inward.

Methodically, instinctively, I began going through emergency procedures.

I pulled out my air bags, inflated them, and tied them to both sides near the stern. I thought briefly about the empty gasoline containers fastened along the side of *Yankee Girl*'s cabin—and then remembered that they'd been torn away yesterday, when we'd capsized. The air bags would have to do.

Afterward I sat and stared at my EPIRB. An orange-and-yellow transmitter about the size of a half-gallon milk carton, my Emergency Position Indicating Radio Beacon was my final card. When—if—I switched it on, it would sent out a continuous tone which would be heard by aircraft on a monitored frequency. They in turn would report it to the Coast Guard, who would request a ship in my area to pick me up.

I shuddered. Even if I did call for help, how would anyone rescue me under these conditions? Trying to get from my boat to a towering steel ship would be more dangerous than staying on board *Yankee Girl*. I visualized a huge black hull, looming 50 feet above me, plunging and wallowing alongside—and, with a final roll, crushing my little plywood vessel.

I could imagine how hard it would be to maneuver a ship in this storm. Moreover, it was highly possible that its crew wouldn't be trained in this kind of rescue attempt.

The odds were not in my favor.

But what would happen if a ship were to come along *right now* and ask, "Do you want to be brought aboard?" What would I do? What would I say?

Sitting in the darkness, I debated with myself. I would have to make a sensible decision—that was clear. But what *was* the best thing to do under these circumstances? I didn't know.

And, finally, what if a ship were to pull up alongside and say, "There's a hurricane coming—the storm is going to get a lot worse"? What then?

I fingered my life jacket, pondering the alternatives.

On the one hand, I was determined not to give up just because I was frightened and miserable. On the other, though, I wanted to act intelligently. Would it be reasonable to stay in the middle of this terrible storm with a hurricane on the way? Would it be worth the risk? Or would it be better to give up my dream, to let myself be rescued by a ship and go back home?

I shook my head, hard. Again I was losing my grip on reality.

For there was no ship. There would be no ship. I was alone, in the here and now, and all I could do was hope to survive.

IX

Overboard!

"The sea never changes and its
works, for all the talk of men,
are wrapped in mystery."
Joseph Conrad

Slowly the storm was dying. Though waves were still racing along at speeds of up to 20 knots, they were now only six to ten feet high and were no longer breaking. After days of shrieking and howling around us, the wind had dropped to a more tolerable 20 knots—and, perversely, swung around to the northwest.

Yankee Girl bobbed downwind with the gray-green rollers. We were moving—an inch at a time, but moving nevertheless.

It was June 15, the fifteenth day of my voyage. Seven days of unbelievably severe weather had left me both mentally and physically drained. I was tired and dirty and miserable. Although I knew that conditions were beginning to improve, I was overcome with frustration.

I peered out a porthole for what seemed like the hundredth time that morning. An eerie white haze hung in the air, and the sun was a luminous slit on the horizon. Heaped up by the shifting wind, swiftly rolling waves heaved and boiled along the ocean's surface.

With growing impatience, I slid open the wooden hatch. I had suffered this storm long enough; I wanted to do some sailing!

As I stuck my head out the hatch, I breathed deeply and smiled for the first time in days. The fresh salt air filled my lungs and sharpened my senses. It felt wonderful to escape from the oppressive, clammy cabin, to feel like a sailor again instead of a mole.

But when I tried to stand up in the hatch, my smile quickly changed to a grimace. My muscles and tendons had been cramped and squeezed for so long that they simply wouldn't function. For a while all I could do was to kneel with my upper body sticking out of the hatchway and my arms braced on the rails. Then, gradually and painfully, I straightened my back and held my body erect at last.

I would have to take my foul-weather gear off soon. My buttocks were chafed raw, the fungus on my groin itched horribly, and I felt slimy everywhere beneath my clothing. That could wait, though. More than anything, I wanted to get the boat going.

I knew that the wind would allow me to carry some canvas, but the speed and height of the waves still intimidated me. I would have to be careful.

As I stretched and looked around at the foredeck, I was relieved to see that the sails were still secure. The two jibs lay furled and strapped down under shock cords, hanked to the forestays with brass snaps. They had withstood the breaking waves and clawing winds—as I had hoped they would. The mainsail, held tightly with shock cord against the boom, seemed to have survived intact, along with the spars and rigging.

In order to hoist the jib, I first had to go forward to the bow, unhook the jibsnap, and release the shock cords. Then I would be able to pull on the halyard and raise the already reefed sail.

Cautiously I climbed out of the hatchway, grabbed the stainless-steel shroud with one hand and the mast with the other, and finally stood upright on the cabin top.

"It's a little like being on a trampoline during an earthquake, isn't it?" my imaginary friend asked mischievously.

"With a 400-pound wrestler jumping up and down on the other end," I answered, grinning.

I spread my feet apart on the hatch cover, thankful for the security of my safety harness and its ⅜-inch dacron lifeline. It had been seven long days since I'd been able to see beyond *Yankee Girl*'s immediate vicinity, and I relished the view.

"Too bad there's nothing to see but waves," my friend gibed.

"When I get tired of them, I'll let you know," I shot back.

Just standing on top of the boat filled me with elation. It was like coming out of a year—no, make that *ten* years—of solitary confinement. I could breathe again!

I paused for a few seconds to plan my next move. Hoisting the jib would be tricky. *Yankee Girl*'s tiny bow didn't have much buoyancy; she would bury her nose in the water when pressed by my weight. I would have to be very careful of my footing—and work fast.

With every muscle tensed and ready to go, I waited for the right moment—a lull between the waves.

Then, over my shoulder, I saw something that made me freeze in terror.

A massive wall of water was roaring toward us. A new northwest wave—a rogue—was crossing over the old system, flattening the other waves as if they had been made of paper.

I hung on to the rigging and stared.

Suddenly I realized that the hatch was still open. Foolishly, I had forgotten to close it when I'd climbed above. Now the wave was towering over it, threatening to fill *Yankee Girl's* cabin.

Frantically I leaned backward with all my weight, hoping to lever the stern up.

The wave slammed into the transom, lifted the stern, and threw it sideways. Water raced to meet me as I clung to the shroud.

For the second time since the beginning of my journey, we were capsizing!

I was plunged into the churning water. Gasping for breath, I watched, horror-struck, as the deck went completely under on the port side. Meanwhile the wave curled menacingly toward the open hatch.

Yankee Girl was now so far down that I could see inside her cabin. If she went any further, or if she were struck by another wave, she could roll all the way over. Then my safety line would wrap itself around her—and I would be trapped below the surface.

Kicking desperately, I struggled against my water-filled clothing. I clenched my hands around the stainless-steel shroud and felt its cold bite.

Then, abruptly, *Yankee Girl* righted herself—pulling me up with her.

Once again my little girl had saved me from my own carelessness.

Everything had happened so quickly that I'd been in the sea for only a few seconds. Luckily, I hadn't even lost my glasses.

I didn't hesitate. With water pouring out of my foul-weather gear, I scrambled below and slammed the hatch shut behind me.

I slumped on my berth, thoroughly shaken and furious with myself.

Again and again I pounded my fist into the seat cushion. How could I have been so stupid? How could I have made such an idiotic mistake? I should have known better than to have my weight up so high in conditions like these!

While I'd been standing on top of the cabin, feeling as if I owned the world, I had taken a chance—a dumb, unforgivable chance that had nearly cost me my life.

I sat there for a long time, raging at myself.

Finally I became aware of my soggy clothing—and my pain. My raw, infected skin, which had been irritated by its unexpected saltwater bath, burned as if it were on fire. The tiny cabin was again full of sea water, and as the waves rolled us about the salt was literally rubbing into my wounds.

In a black mood, I rummaged around up forward until I found what I was looking for: a clean shirt and a pair of tan work pants. I stripped off my wet clothing and patted myself dry with a towel. Then I dusted talcum powder over my inflamed skin to reduce the chafing.

My pants hung loosely around my waist. In my 15 days at sea I had lost about ten pounds.

There was no way I could wash or dry my old clothes, so I threw them overboard, knowing that they would eventually disintegrate.

I felt better after I'd dried myself off and changed my clothes, but I stayed inside the cabin anyway. I vowed that I wouldn't go above again until the next morning; I had to prove that I was still capable of disciplining myself. Besides, I needed time to think about the blunder I'd made—and learn what I could from it.

Outside, the weather steadily improved.

The next morning dawned breezy but sunny. Overnight the wind had swung to the north-northeast—perfect for a beam reach to the east. Best of all, the waves had settled down to heights of between four and five feet. Compared to the monsters that had battered us during the storm, they seemed like ripples on a pond.

Still unnerved by my unexpected dunking of the day before, I went forward to hoist the reefed jib. As I hauled in the sheets, I drew in *Yankee Girl*'s sails to the taut curves that would power her effortlessly along. With an exhilarating surge, she sliced through the water.

For the first time in eight days we were sailing a course for England.

"Looks like your luck is changing, Ger," my imaginary friend remarked.

"We'll make it yet, old buddy," I replied.

I was actually feeling cheerful. Earlier that might have made me incautious, but now I knew better. Even though it would have been delightful to sail with the hatch open, I kept it closed to seal out the spray.

The weather was so favorable that I decided to let *Yankee Girl* steer herself. I brought the starboard jib sheet into the cabin, passed it through a block, and pulled the end back to the tiller. The resulting tension was balanced out by two pieces of surgical tubing connected to the tiller from the opposite side.

This arrangement allowed *Yankee Girl* to continue moving on her present course, but relative to the wind. And—as I was both surprised and humbled to discover—it freed her to sail both straighter and faster than if I were steering her.

There was one disadvantage to my self-steering setup: it encroached upon my little domain. Because of the lines stretching across to the tiller, I could no longer sit with my back against the transom. Nor could I use my special tiller seat, since that would also interfere with the lines. I couldn't even stick my feet inside the footwell, for it was still overflowing with gear—30 to 40 issues of *Reader's Digest*, a pair of shoes, spare lumber, a bucket, and more of that ever-present grapefruit.

After doing some experimenting, I found that I was most comfortable stretched across the cabin in a semi-reclining position. I couldn't see the water from there, but I had the rather pleasant sensation of riding in a racing 12-meter yacht. And I enjoyed the sound of the waves—and the miles—rushing by.

I didn't like sailing completely blind, so every once in a while I rose up, slid back the hatch, and scoured the horizon for ships. I didn't expect to see any, but it didn't hurt to check.

If and when the seas calmed down to the point where I could leave the hatch open, I'd have a long list of chores to tackle. For the moment, though, there was nothing for me to do but lie back, relax, and let the boat steer herself.

I was intrigued by my simple arrangement of blocks, lines, and tubing, and I spent hours staring at it, trying to figure out how it managed to steer the boat more efficiently than I could. I also took pleasure in watching my compass mirror my little yacht's progress through the water. We were heading east, or 110 degrees magnetic. Whenever *Yankee Girl* hit a wave the needle would veer over toward 120 degrees, slide back up to 100 degrees, and finally settle on 110 again.

Under sail and steering herself, *Yankee Girl* zipped along for three days and three nights at near hull speed.

Slowly but surely, we both recuperated from the storm. We'd come through it in good shape with amazingly few losses: the gas cans I'd strapped on deck, and the sea anchor. I'd never been able to determine the source of the cracking noise I'd heard, and eventually I stopped worrying about it. The boat seemed structurally sound, and there was no sea water in the bilges.

Sometimes I listened to the radio. The Canadian Broadcasting Corporation's programs were my favorites. In the mornings they'd be in English, but later in the day they'd alternate between French and either Cree or Angokok—Indian and Inuk dialects. Even though I had no idea what the afternoon announcers were saying, I liked the company of their friendly voices.

I began forcing myself to eat regularly. For now the weather was good and the sailing was easy, but I had no guarantee that these conditions would last, and I couldn't afford to lose any more weight or strength. My appetite had improved, too; even the grapefruit I had been sleeping on looked appealing.

I busied myself with my charts in an attempt to fix my position. In the past I'd relied for the most part on rough, imprecise sights—the best I could come up with when *Yankee Girl* was gyrating wildly through the waves. On the nineteenth day of my voyage, I finally took what I considered to be accurate altitudes.

As I worked through the calculations, I found that I was at 38 degrees 48 minutes N, 56 degrees 50 minutes W.

I had covered one-fourth of the distance to England.

Somehow, in spite of bad weather, I had gone more than 825 nautical miles in 19 days. This was encouraging—until I averaged the figures out and discovered that I'd been traveling only 43 miles per day. I was still behind schedule.

As the days wore on, I longed more and more for a period of calm. I had a great deal to do, and I was beginning to feel frustrated by the waves which were preventing me from getting to work.

I wanted to check my motor, which had been hit hard by the storm. Though I'd pulled the starting cord through several times, it hadn't even coughed; I wondered whether it would ever start again. I was also eager to nail down the nylon transom flap that had let in so much water during the storm. And I needed to get food out of the forward compartments and look over the bilges.

While I waited for the seas to die down, I made minor adjustments to the boat. One day, after a brief rain, I unhooked the anchor line and brought it into the cabin. Normally I kept it attached to an eye at the bow, always at the ready, but out here it didn't really seem to matter. I doubted whether the anchor would have much effect in 20,000 feet of water!

By the twenty-third day my fix indicated that I had come more than 1,200 miles, or about one-third of the way. I had about 2,500 miles left to go. With the storm only a bad memory and *Yankee Girl* making excellent progress, England once again seemed a reality.

The Gulf Stream was carrying us slowly northward, closer to the shipping lanes. We would soon be entering an area of very heavy traffic, that part of the North Atlantic in which ships "turned the corner" to avoid icebergs coming down from the north. We'd be within the iceberg limit, but I didn't expect to see any of these floating mountains. Nor did I want to. I felt the same way about them as I did about tornadoes: it would be a tremendous thrill to see one, but I didn't relish the idea of one coming at me.

After three weeks at sea, the constant isolation was making me tense and edgy. Little things were getting on my nerves. One day, for example, I was fumbling around for a piece of candy when I somehow bumped the button on my foghorn. The loud *bl-a-a-a-at* made me jump.

"Now *that* was funny," my friend chuckled. "Do it again."

I still wasn't getting more than an hour of uninterrupted sleep at a time. Often I'd just be dropping off when a midnight squall would rouse me out of my bunk to douse the sails. And I hadn't yet found a truly comfortable position inside the cramped cabin. My fatigue was beginning to show, and I knew it. Because of it I was becoming slightly careless again.

One morning I decided to breakfast on granola for the first time during my voyage. As I bent over the stern to wash my red plastic bowl, I dropped it. I knelt there helplessly and watched it float away. I might have been able to turn *Yankee Girl* around, go back, and retrieve it, but I was simply too tired.

At least we were making good progress; by now we were averaging 60 nautical miles per day. Though I kept the hatch closed because of the spray—that wouldn't stop being a problem until the waves subsided—I was able to leave the drop board out and get some fresh air.

I'd watch the compass for hours at a time, mesmerized by its deliberate, predictable movements. We'd be at 80 degrees, then 90, and we'd hit a wave and slip back to 80. Or we'd be at 90, then 100, and we'd heel and return to 90 again.

Under the prevailing conditions, 100 degrees was as far as we could go to the east. Since the magnetic variation in this part of world was running at about 20 degrees west, we needed to sail 110 degrees by the compass in order to go due east. But the little bit of northing we were making wasn't hurting us that much.

I was primarily concerned with staying south of the shipping lanes, away from the possibility of collision. Occasionally I'd scan the horizon for ships, just in case.

I hadn't seen a ship for nearly two weeks, though. It seemed as if I had the Atlantic all to myself. In fact, I was growing accustomed to being alone, to believing that I probably wouldn't see another ship for quite some time.

Another bit of carelessness I'd live to regret.

I got into the habit of eating my evening meal early. I'd have my pan and spoon washed and put away in time for one of the highlights of my day: the sunset. I'd gaze at that glorious spectacle, relishing every last hue and ray of light, and then slink into my little cavern of a cabin and slide the hatch shut.

Immediately after sunset the air cooled, and the moisture that the sun had drawn upward during the day suddenly descended in heavy condensation. I knew that if I left the hatch open everything inside the cabin would be saturated within a few minutes. I missed being able to watch the night fall over the ocean, but I always forced myself to close the hatch.

During the next hour or so I usually listened to my tape recorder and sang along with Linda Ronstadt or the Powdermilk Biscuit Band, a Minnesota group. Somehow music had the power to waft me home, to carry me back to the pines and birches and sparkling blue lakes.

I spent many evenings lying curled up on my bunk, dreaming about my family and friends. Often I imagined that someone I loved suddenly appeared out of nowhere and greeted me with a kiss, or put an arm around my shoulder, or just sat down beside me and asked me how I was. These flights of fantasy were therapeutic and formed my only means of fighting off my withering loneliness. Afterward I slept peacefully, rocked by my little boat's gentle motion.

One night I awoke, poked my head out of the hatch to look for ships, and then lay down for another hour's rest. I glanced at my watch; it was 9:30 P.M.

At 10:30 my inner alarm woke me again. I started to move toward the hatch—and stopped. I hadn't seen a ship for days, and the chances that I would now, at this very minute, were slim. Besides, I was hungry. I'd eat now—and check later.

With a practiced motion, I turned on my small battery-powered cabin light and rummaged through my provisions until I found a can of peaches. Then I opened it and reached for my spoon.

The glow from my radio dial would provide me with plenty of light to eat by, and it seemed silly to waste batteries, so I turned off the cabin light.

I sat back, utterly relaxed, and started digging into the can.

All at once *Yankee Girl*'s cabin was flooded by light streaming in through her portholes. For one wild moment I thought that a spaceship had landed directly on top of us.

I heaved the hatch open in alarm and stared in disbelief as a towering wall of steel slid by only a hundred feet away. Blinded by the ship's lights, which reflected off the water in every direction, I could see nothing on her deck. She may as well have been a spaceship, for a visitor from another planet wouldn't have surprised me nearly as much.

At least she had missed us.

But what if she had come up behind us?

Trembling, I dove for my radio.

"WXQ 9864 . . . WXQ 9864 . . . This is the yacht *Yankee*

Girl calling any ship in the area . . . This is the yacht *Yankee Girl* calling any ship in the area . . . Over."

The response came immediately.

"*Yankee Girl, Yankee Girl*, this is the *African Comet*. We were surprised to see your light."

What light? What were they talking about?

"You really gave me a start," I answered. "Didn't you pick me up on radar?"

"Negative on the radar. We saw your light and tried to miss you."

Then the realization hit me. The only light they could have seen was the tiny cabin light I'd turned on for a few moments—and turned off again.

I was astounded—and badly shaken.

What would have happened if I'd slept only five minutes more?

X

Day of Calm

"Alone, alone, all, all alone;
Alone on a wide, wide sea."
Samuel Taylor Coleridge

By 9 A.M. on the morning of June 29, the sun was already high over the softly undulating ocean. The waves were gone, and the ever-present swells beneath the surface lapped gently at *Yankee Girl*'s hull.

It was going to be a perfect day. Golden sunshine, blue skies, and a peaceful indigo sea—exactly the sort of day I had been waiting for.

As I awoke and stretched, I couldn't help but think of how nice it would be to spend a few hours at the beach, to lie on the sand and not have to worry about a thing. Somewhere people were probably doing just that; I was the only person in the world who was sitting in the middle of the Atlantic in a ten-foot boat.

I glanced at my watch. I had slept for three solid hours—the longest uninterrupted period of rest I'd had in nearly a month. At some time during the night *Yankee Girl*'s up-and-down motion had changed to a gentle rocking, lulling me into a lengthy morning nap.

After so many days of being tossed about by the wind and waves, I was not prepared for the almost palpable silence. All of the noises I'd grown accustomed to hearing were absent—from the slap of the halyards against the mast to the rattle of gear in the lockers. Even the familiar gurgle of water under the hull had been stilled.

Slowly unkinking my body, I stared out the hatchway, thoroughly enjoying the view.

The North Atlantic was in one of her rare benign moods, and she was beautiful. At rest, she resembled a limitless ballroom, a gleaming blue plain that extended in every direction. I had to suppress the urge to jump out of the boat and run wildly across the water; I would have given almost anything for the chance to walk a few steps and exercise my stiff legs.

I couldn't dawdle any longer. Already my three-hour nap had put me behind schedule, and I wanted to make the most of this day. I'd finally have the opportunity to tackle some of the little jobs I'd wanted to do for weeks. A compulsive list-maker, I'd been writing down everything that occurred to me, and watching my list grow and grow had filled me with frustration. Now I'd be able to shorten it.

As I scrambled my breakfast eggs, I went over all of the things I'd try to do during the next several hours. First I'd check the motor. Then I'd lubricate the sliding hatch cover and transfer some food and fuel. Later I'd reward myself with a bath.

Immediately after washing my dishes, I began working on the outboard. I had been worried about it for some time. During the past weeks it had been hammered by hundreds of waves and occasionally immersed completely as it hung on its bracket. Cross-waves had hit it so hard that I'd heard it shudder, and I had often peered out my inspection port to see whether it was still there.

I unscrewed the clamps, hoisted the 40-pound Evinrude up, and set it on the half-open hatch cover. After slipping a couple of squares of paper towel beneath it, I reached for the biggest screwdriver in my tool kit. Then I unscrewed the metal plug on the lower unit.

A trickle of oil flowed onto the white paper. It was thick and clear. There was no sign of the sea water that would cause the gears to bind and the shaft to seize. After replacing the plug, I carefully swung the motor back over the stern and secured it to its bracket.

Next I removed the power head cowling to check for rust. The starting mechanism and coils were corroded, so I sprayed them with lubricant and wiped them clean. When I unscrewed the spark plugs from the cylinders, I saw that they were heavily carboned but dry. Quickly I screwed in two new plugs from the ten spare sets I had on board.

I paused to wipe beads of perspiration from my forehead. The sun was getting hotter, and I was starting to itch. I'd been wearing the same clothing for days, and the idea of a bath was becoming an obsession.

As I turned to put my wrench back in the toolbox, I glanced overhead.

There, like a giant white plume against the azure sky, was a jet's contrail.

I stared in envy as I reflected on those two hundred or more passengers up there who were merrily eating and drinking their way to London. None of them could see me, of course, but I found it comforting just to know that there were other human beings around.

I watched until the aircraft was out of sight. Its contrail lingered, miles above my mast; I took it as a good omen.

Scratching my month-old beard, I turned my attention back

to the motor. Starting it, I knew, was going to be a problem. After all, it had been hanging there unused—and abused—for three long weeks.

I crossed my fingers and pulled the starting cord through. But it would not rewind; its recoil spring was rusted. I sprayed it with oil and pulled it through again to get the gas up.

By the seventh pull, it hadn't even coughed.

This was not a good sign. If I couldn't get the motor running, I wouldn't be able to avoid the ships in the calms that lay ahead. My position would become increasingly precarious as I approached the English Channel with its heavy traffic and strong currents. I *had* to have power for both safety and maneuverability.

I looked up at the "good luck" contrail once and yanked the cord again and again.

With a rasp that was music to my ears, the little engine sputtered into life. I resisted the impulse to hug it and instead turned up the throttle to warm it up. Then I ran it for 15 minutes at speed.

When I was certain that the motor was all right, I turned it off and consulted my "to do" list to determine my next project.

I was still concerned about the strange cracking noise I'd heard during the height of the storm. Although I'd checked the bilges repeatedly, I hadn't been able to find any sign of damage. The hull appeared to be sound, and no water was coming in.

Perhaps the fiberglass sheathing around the hull had been weakened or harmed in some way. If so, it could eventually flex and crack, allowing sea water to leak into the plywood and cause delamination.

I was also worried about the lower gudgeon that held the base of the rudder. Though I could detect no flex at the tiller, I knew that the fittings had taken a beating from the breakers.

I would simply have to give the boat a thorough going over, and there was only one way to do it.

I searched through my gear until I found my mask and snorkel. Then I stripped off my clothing and, for the first time since the beginning of my voyage, unsnapped my safety harness.

Climbing onto the cabin top, I peered into the water. I needed to know what was down there.

The water was so full of plankton that its surface was dimpled. A foot or so below it, little maroon and silver fish zoomed about. They had been following us for days. Now, as I leaned over them, they darted out of sight beneath *Yankee Girl*'s motionless hull.

Long, tubular jellyfish, some colored red or yellow at one end, drifted through the water on all sides of the boat. They appeared to be harmless, but I couldn't be sure. On the other hand, I knew that the garish reddish-blue creatures dotting the surface around us could inflict a serious sting. They were Portuguese men-of-war, their pneumatic sails raised in anticipation of a breeze, and they would bear watching.

As I rested against the mast, gazing out over the endless sea, I became aware that the only sounds I heard were the ones I made. In the absence of wind, the ocean was utterly silent. The marine life slid by without a whisper. It was a curious sensation; I felt almost as if I were in a vacuum and sounds were being sucked out of me to fill that limitless void.

Experimentally, I began to shout and whistle, but each new noise I made just floated away. There was nothing to echo it back to me.

Again I realized how insignificant I was, how small a part I played in the universe.

I went back to studying the water. I couldn't see any sharks, but that didn't mean there weren't any around. In certain areas of the ocean, like the one I was in, passing vessels regularly tossed garbage and scraps overboard, and the local sharks were used to handouts. Any boat, even one as tiny as mine, would draw them like a dinner bell.

Satisfied that the area looked safe, I donned my mask and

snorkel. Then, after one more glance into the water, I jumped into the sea with a splash.

As soon as my head went below the surface, I spun around and checked in every direction for uninvited company. Seeing nothing alarming, I relaxed for a moment.

Beneath its plankton layer, the water was surprisingly clear. The temperature was in the 70s—very comfortable against my bare skin. I felt as if I'd been submerged in a huge bowl of tepid soup.

I looked up at *Yankee Girl*'s blue bottom. From this perspective, even she looked like a shark.

I rose to the surface, took a breath, and dove under the boat once more. I moved along beneath it, running my fingers along the garboard where the planking joined the skeg.

I'd been afraid that I'd find the hull seriously damaged. But now, as I looked and felt my way along, I was relieved to discover that there were no cracks or holes. The bottom was perfect—as sound as it had been back in Minnesota.

I had to smile at my own foolishness. For weeks my imagination had been working overtime; I'd spent hours envisioning all kinds of terrible things. I should have known better than to lose confidence in my little girl.

Out of breath again, I headed for the surface on the other side of the boat. By this time I was so apprehensive about sharks that I hauled myself directly up and out of the water. Back on deck, I realized that I hadn't even thought about the rudder fitting.

I had gotten spooked—and perhaps with good cause. A shark wouldn't have to bite off my leg to disable or kill me; even a little nibble could do me in. I reminded myself that sharks almost never attack people—and, when they do, they seldom take more than a sample and then spit it out. But this thought wasn't very comforting.

I knelt on the deck, hesitating. I wanted to go back down to check the rudder fitting, but I also wanted to stay on my boat where I knew I'd be safe.

Suddenly I remembered the bath I'd been promising myself

all morning. Somehow that took precedence over my fear of sharks.

I reached into the cabin and brought out my bottle of Joy dishwashing detergent—an all-purpose liquid that, in my mind at least, was far more effective than so-called saltwater soap. With one foot on the deck and the other on the cabin top, I happily began sudsing myself, humming aloud. Soon I was covered in lather and ready for a rinse. Now I had two reasons to reenter the water.

But again I hesitated. If I jumped overboard, I would make another big splash. Sharks were attracted to that kind of noise—or to anything thrashing about in the water. To them, that signaled wounded prey.

I braced myself, inhaled deeply, and dove. Immediately after rising to the surface, I swam to the transom step and hauled myself up, naked and dripping, to the deck.

For the second time I had forgotten to inspect the rudder, but there was nothing that could induce me to go back into the water. Two periods of eerie uncertainty had been enough. I'd have to examine it later, from the surface, using my diving mask.

I grabbed the bucket and finished rinsing myself on deck. Then I toweled myself off as quickly as I could. This was the secret of a successful "sea bath"—getting the salt water off before it had the chance to dry and leave a sticky residue. Next I poured a cup of fresh water from one of my containers, dipped paper towels into it, and wiped off my body. Afterward I slowly trickled the rest of the water down my back and chest.

Clean at last! I felt wonderful. Refreshed. Almost civilized.

As I stood naked on the deck with the hot sun beating down my back, I glanced nervously over my shoulder.

"See anybody?" my imaginary friend asked.

I had to laugh. Here I was, about as far from other people as I could get, and I was worried that someone might catch me without my clothes on!

I decided to remain in my pristine state for a while longer.

Maybe the sunshine and fresh air would have a healing effect on my raw skin. By now my fungus infection was extremely painful. On some parts of my body, particularly the area around my groin, the skin was literally peeling away—the result of too many days in soggy foul-weather gear. The exposure would do it good.

I donned a T-shirt and my safety harness, but that was all. Then, after a brief rest, I returned to my list of things to do.

My next priority was the nylon cover over the tiller opening—the one that had let in so much water during the storm. If I could succeed in sealing it off, future gales wouldn't pose such a threat.

I got out my hammer and two dozen nails, held the brads in place against the transom with needle-nosed pliers, and nailed the flap down—permanently. It seemed like such an obvious solution that I was annoyed with myself for not coming up with it sooner. If I'd thought of it before leaving Virginia, my life at sea would have been a lot easier.

Next I wanted to improve my system of reefing the foresails. The way things were now, I had to go all the way to the bow to set the reduced jibs. That was what had led to my untimely trip over the side several days ago.

With a couple of lines and cam cleats, I devised an arrangement that allowed me to pull the jibs down to the reefed position from the safety of the hatchway. When I tried it out, it worked perfectly. I'd never again have to endanger myself or *Yankee Girl* by going forward during a storm.

Satisfied, I turned my attention to some minor problems I was having with fittings. The empty gasoline containers that had been ripped away during the storm had been fastened to the hull by a deck strap, and that too had been torn off. I replaced it, using longer screws and driving them well into the deck stringer.

I also replaced the rivets holding the lower whisker pole. The combination of aluminum rivets, a brass fitting, and a constant saltwater bath had been the perfect environment for electrolysis, which had eventually dissolved the fastenings.

I noticed that one of the aluminum screws holding my cabin-top compass was broken. At first I thought that the screw had been cracked when the mainsheet had caught on the compass, but a closer examination revealed that it was another victim of electrolysis. After removing the aluminum screws, I fastened the compass down with new brass ones.

By this time the sun was almost overhead, and its rays were becoming intense. It seemed wise to work below for a while.

There were two jobs on my list that could be taken care of simultaneously: transferring gasoline to the main tank, and retrieving some of the food that was stored up in the bow.

In order to get to the forward lockers, I had to move everything in the bow to the stern. I squirmed through my gear like a mole, passing sleeping bags, clothing, books, and cans down toward my feet as I went. Once I made it to the bow, I couldn't move back without reversing the procedure and pulling all of my gear forward again. What would ordinarily have taken five minutes took nearly an hour, and when I finally finished I was dripping with sweat in the 90-degree heat of the cabin.

I was getting hungrier by the minute, but it was almost local noon, and I wanted to take a sight before I sat down to eat. After carefully unshipping one of my plastic Davis sextants, I wedged myself across the companionway and aimed the sextant toward the south. I squinted into the eyepiece, brought the sun down to the horizon, and noted the angle.

To make sure that I had caught the sun at its zenith, I took a series of sights. Then I worked out the calculations. I discovered that we were at 41 degrees 05 minutes N—a bit farther north than I wanted to be, but not enough to cause concern.

At last I could relax and enjoy a leisurely lunch. It had been a busy morning; I was pleased with what I had accomplished. On top of everything else, I'd even gotten to take a bath. I felt better than I had since the beginning of my journey.

While foraging through the forward lockers, I'd discovered several cans of asparagus. I opened one of these, along with a can of corn and a can of tuna. I jazzed up the tuna with salt, pepper, and fresh lemon juice. Finally—I was really splurging now—I opened a bottle of Pepsi.

I spread my feast out on the hatch cover and stood in the companionway, relishing the moment.

"How's this for a picnic?" I asked my friend.

"Great," he replied. "We've got everything but the ants."

After lunch, as the temperature continued to rise, I opened my umbrella to ward off the sun's rays. It covered the hatch neatly. When I tilted it up a little on the forward side, it even scooped up some air and sent it my way as we motored along.

I'd decided to get moving again, and the Evinrude was working like a charm. Sometimes, just to break the monotony, I sung along with its constant roar, raising my voice in attempted harmony.

With the tiller lashed dead center, I was trying to hold a course of 110 degrees magnetic. Though the outboard was angled slightly inward to compensate for its off-center position, I had to keep a close eye on the compass, checking my position every few seconds and making corrections as necessary.

The best way to do this, I discovered, was to shift my shoulders on the bunk or lean slightly to one side. While motoring on such a calm sea, *Yankee Girl* steered better if I moved my body than if I adjusted the tiller.

For the rest of the afternoon, we chugged steadily over the glassy blue Atlantic. It was utterly empty and utterly peaceful. The water stretched endlessly from horizon to horizon, where sea and sky met in a hazy blur.

Although I was alone, I couldn't help but notice that others had been here before me. The surface of the water was littered with styrofoam cups, wooden crates, pillows, sheets of plastic, oil drums, and the ever-present globules of crude oil.

Just after sunset, the wind came up out of the southwest at about 11 to 16 knots. I was delighted. This was what the prevailing wind should have been from the very beginning! All that night and the following day, we sailed under *Yankee Girl*'s self-steering mechanism. She did the work; I read and relaxed.

It was a great way to spend my thirtieth day at sea.

> *"Don't you wanna . . ."*
> *". . . like to . . ."*
> *". . . Ger . . ."*
> *". . . are you . . ."*

The voices came through the sides of the boat from somewhere out on the water. I sat very still for a moment, listening and wondering.

They continued to chatter eerily, like ghosts calling weakly from afar; always in snatches of words or phrases, never in complete sentences.

I shivered in the gathering darkness. This was not the first time I'd heard voices during my journey. I *knew* there was no one out there, but the strange babbling sounds still raised the hairs on the back of my neck.

Was I losing my grip on reality? It had happened to plenty of other single-handers. Many of them had reported becoming temporarily deranged from the isolation and loneliness, and I was afraid that the same thing was happening to me.

> *". . . Ger . . ."*

Forcing myself up, I peered out over the transom.

"Is there anybody out there?" my friend inquired.

"Not in our immediate vicinity," I answered.

Now all I heard was the burbling of the water in *Yankee Girl*'s turbulent wake. The physical act of getting up had cleared my head.

I was aware of what was happening, of course. I was out in

the middle of nowhere, alone on the ocean, and my mind was trying to create some company for me. The only real conversation going on at the moment was the one between my *Yankee Girl* and the sea.

I retreated into the cabin and turned on my multi-band radio. For a while I listened to some Spanish guitar music broadcast by radio Madrid, but that offered little consolation. So I got out my tape recorder and sang along with the Ink Spots' rendition of *I Cover the Waterfront*.

The sound of my voice filled the tiny cabin, and I no longer felt like a castaway.

When I finally tired of singing, I switched off the tape player and opened a can of peaches. As I ate my late-night snack in the open hatch, I stared in fascination at the countless stars spread out above me.

Suddenly something hit me in the face like a wet hand.

Almost instinctively, I pushed the switch on the overhead light and looked around. There in the footwell, wriggling and flopping from side to side, was a small flying fish. I reached for a Kleenex and made a grab for the fish as it skittered among the shoes, spare wood, and books. Finally I caught it and flipped it overboard.

At least the fish had been real.

Afterward I sat in the hatch for a long time, gazing at the sea. The Atlantic was more beautiful tonight than I had ever seen her. Phosphorescence spread out behind us like a trail of sequined milk, with individual flecks mirroring the stars overhead. It was so bright that it illuminated *Yankee Girl*'s hull.

It almost seemed as if the world had been turned upside-down and we were sailing the heavens like a comet, leaving a shimmering tail behind us. Even my finny mascots left glowing streaks in the water as they darted in and out beneath us.

I took special delight in watching the jellyfish bobbing in our wake like countless luminous parachutes.

At about 11 P.M., on one of my regular hourly inspections, I saw a ship's lights off on the horizon. I scrambled to my radio and gave them a call. To my surprise, they responded immediately.

"Where are you?" a voice asked. Obviously the crew hadn't yet seen me.

"You're bearing 50 degrees," I answered. "There's a strobe light at my masthead."

There was a pause.

"We see you now," the voice said, "but not very well. Is that your only light?"

"Yes, but my boat is pretty small. Only ten feet."

"Really?" the voice asked incredulously. "How many in the crew?"

"Well, there's only room for one."

Another pause.

"Can you give us a repeat on your length?" came the voice. By now, I could tell, their curiosity was growing.

"Ten feet, and 30 days out of Norfolk, Virginia."

A longer pause.

"Where are you bound?"

"Falmouth, England. Would you be kind enough to give me a position check?"

"It will take a couple of minutes. We'll get back to you."

I waited for what seemed like a long time, becoming increasingly nervous. I was afraid that we'd get cut off in mid-conversation as the distance between us increased, and I still wanted to give them a message to relay back home.

I was relieved to hear the voice once again.

"*Yankee Girl*, we make our position to be 41 degrees 41 minutes north, 40 degrees 33 minutes west."

"Thank you," I said warmly. Then I asked them to do me another favor.

"Would you mind reporting me to the Coast Guard at Portsmouth, Virginia?"

"We'll do it on our schedule."

That meant that they'd probably do it sometime during the next morning, at a predetermined hour when they made their regular calls.

I went all out and made a final request.

"Is there a possibility of calling back to the States on single-side band?"

"Just a minute. We'll have to get our radio operator up here."

Soon a cheery British voice came over the airwaves.

"Hello, *Yankee Girl*. Sparks here."

"Good evening. I'm wondering if it would be possible to call back to the States."

"Sorry," he said, sounding genuinely concerned. "Can't do. We have only code equipment."

In other words, all they could do was send messages by Morse code—the old-fashioned way.

"That's all right; thanks anyway."

I was disappointed that I couldn't get a voice message home, but I double-checked with Sparks about reporting me to the Coast Guard and he assured me that he would. That was something.

We chatted for several minutes more, swapping information. I learned that I was talking with the *Josepha*, an English ship bound from northern Spain with a general cargo for the States.

When our conversation came to an end, I stood in the hatchway and watched the *Josepha* glide slowly into the darkness. Then I went below and unfolded my chart.

I plotted the position I had been given and found that it compared favorably with my own sights. Incredibly, I was only 33 miles from the halfway point.

By morning I would reach the very center of the North Atlantic ocean.

But what would I do then? Head straight for Falmouth—or turn southeast toward the Azores?

For some time I had privately been considering stopping off at the Portuguese islands for a brief rest. According to my chart, they lay only 400 miles away. Currently we were making about 70 miles per day. If I wanted to I could be in Flores, the northernmost island of the Azore Archipelago, in five and one-half days. There I could stretch my aching legs, relax, talk to someone besides myself, eat something that didn't come out of a can, and call home.

It was *very* tempting.

On the other hand, there was nothing I needed in the way of provisions or repairs, and I had just sent a message home via the *Josepha*. If I steered for Falmouth, I would be sticking to my original plan of sailing nonstop across the Atlantic.

Regardless of my decision, I'd be sailing "downhill" after tomorrow. The worst of the voyage *had* to be over. How wonderful it would be to aim for a real port, a final destination!

I made up my mind.

Tomorrow I would set my course for England.

XI

Race for Falmouth

The telephone was ringing when Sally walked in the door. As she picked up the receiver, she glanced at the clock: 6:15 P.M.

It had been a long, hard day. Mondays were always difficult, but this one had seemed worse than most.

"Mrs. Spiess?" a woman's voice asked politely. Then she introduced herself.

Another newspaper reporter.

Sally knew without being asked what the woman wanted: any information on Gerry's whereabouts.

Normally Sally didn't mind reporters calling, and she didn't object to sharing with them any news she had. But tonight she was tired. And besides, she didn't have any news. The last message she'd received from Gerry had been radioed back on June 30 from the *Josepha*.

It was now July 16. Sixteen days without a word.

"There's nothing new," Sally explained wearily. "In fact, we haven't heard anything since the end of June, which is pretty unusual."

The familiar click of a typewriter sounded in the background as the reporter began her article.

"Gerry has generally been prompt," Sally continued. "Usually we've gotten some message back every week to ten days."

There was a pause. When the reporter spoke again, her words carried a certain inflection that Sally was becoming accustomed to.

"Are you getting concerned?" the woman asked.

It was a polite way of asking whether something might have happened at sea and Sally was about to become a widow.

"No," Sally answered, "I'm only concerned that I'll be in England when he arrives there."

She had replied with more conviction than she felt; it was a carefully rehearsed answer. Gerry had been at sea a long time between transmissions, and this last break in communications worried her deeply.

She never really questioned whether Gerry and *Yankee Girl* would make it, but there was always a gnawing question in the back of her mind: *where were they?*

She hated the constant uncertainty, the waiting. She had buried herself in her work, and friends and co-workers had helped to keep her spirits up, but she still experienced periods of intense loneliness and doubt.

Ever since learning of Gerry's departure, the news media had shown only casual interest, apparently taking a wait-and-see attitude. Following Gerry's instructions, Sally had not initiated any contacts. But some reporters—like this one—had come to her.

"Well, thanks very much for your time," the woman finally said.

"Of course . . . you're welcome," Sally replied as she hung up the receiver.

By the morning of July 18—two days later—Sally couldn't stand it any longer. Usually she waited for the Coast Guard station at Portsmouth, Virginia to call her. But it had been 18 days since the last message—far too long. She decided to break with tradition and call them.

It was 6:45 A.M. when Sally dialed the coordination area.

"Coast Guard Station, Portsmouth," the duty officer answered crisply.

"Good morning, I'm Sally Spiess. I'm anxious to know whether you have heard anything from my husband Gerry and *Yankee Girl.*"

"Yes. As a matter of fact, we were just about to call you."

While Sally waited for the officer to retrieve the message, she reached for her chart of the North Atlantic.

In a moment he was back on the line.

"*Yankee Girl* was sighted by the *Potomac* at 10 A.M. Greenwich Mean Time, location 48 degrees 58 minutes north, 16 degrees 20 minutes west . . . ."

As the officer continued to speak, Sally excitedly pinpointed the coordinates he'd given her.

Then she stopped and stared at her chart.

Gerry was now less than 475 miles from Falmouth. In the two and a half weeks since she'd last heard from him, he had made incredible progress. It almost seemed as if he had *jumped* across the ocean.

She had to get to England before he did—but there were so many things to do before then. Like buying travelers' checks, changing her airline tickets, packing her suitcases, finishing up work at the office, putting the house and garden in order. . . .

Feeling slightly dazed, Sally thanked the officer for his help.

She hung up the phone, picked it up again, and immediately dialed Gerry's parents.

His father answered.

"Lou, I've just received a message from Gerry," Sally said breathlessly. "You'll never guess how far he's gotten!"

"Great!" Lou said. "Let me get a pencil!"

Sally gave him the coordinates and waited while he plotted Gerry's position.

"Well, this *is* good news!" he finally said. "We'll have to make new flight reservations right away."

"That's not all that needs to be done," Sally answered.

They talked for a while longer, making plans.

Afterward she glanced again at the kitchen clock. It was now 7:20 A.M. She was running far behind schedule, and the traffic would be peaking at this hour. Sighing, she finished getting ready for work.

When she arrived at her office an hour later, Sally went straight to the large map of the Atlantic which hung on the wall behind her desk. Stretching across it was a red line indicating Gerry's course. Each sighting was marked with the time, date, and reporting vessel.

Sally picked up her red pen, drew in the coordinates she had just received, and connected them with the previous ones. Once again she was amazed to see how far Gerry had traveled during the last several days.

He was *very* close to England. Maybe only a week away.

As usual, Sally's co-workers began coming in to find out whether she'd received any news.

"Look at where he is!" she said proudly, pointing toward the map.

"That's wonderful, Sal," said Bill Beilharz. "Now you can start scheduling things."

He sounded relieved—and so did her other co-workers. Everyone in the office had been walking on eggshells ever since Gerry had left for England over a month and a half ago.

At about 11 A.M. the telephone on Sally's desk rang.

"Sally, this is Larry," a voice said.

Larry Maddry, a newspaper reporter in Virginia Beach, was a friend of Gerry's. He had written the article transmitted by the Associated Press on June 12, the day after Gerry had been sighted by the Dutch ship *Bilderdyk*. Along with the rest of Gerry's friends on the coast, he had been following the solo crossing closely.

"Did you hear from the Coast Guard?" Larry asked.

"Yes. Isn't it fantastic?" Sally answered.

"Can you make it over that soon?"

"What do you mean, that soon?"

"Sally, he'll be arriving in Falmouth on Sunday."

"*Sunday*! Where did you hear that?"

"Didn't the Coast Guard tell you that his estimated time of arrival is July 22?"

Sally couldn't believe what she was hearing. She also couldn't believe that the Coast Guard hadn't told her that date. Then she remembered—she had been so busy plotting the new coordinates that she hadn't listened very closely to the rest of what the officer had said.

"I guess I missed that part," she confessed. "But are you certain?"

"Yes, I just talked with them."

"Thanks, Larry. Call me later if you hear anything else."

Louis Spiess picked up his telephone on the second ring.

"Are you sitting down?" Sally asked.

"I am now," he answered. "What's up?"

"I just got the rest of the Coast Guard message. Gerry's expected to arrive on Sunday!"

"Oh my gosh. We'll have to change everything again so we can leave on Friday."

"Do you think we can make it?" Sally wanted to know. She felt numb.

"Of course we can," Lou said.

———————————— ⚓ ————————————

By 8:30 A.M. on Thursday, July 19, Jason Davis was already at his desk in the KSTP-TV newsroom in Minneapolis. As he sipped his first cup of black coffee, he casually scanned the morning mail, newspapers, assignment sheets, and clippings. He took in most of it in a glance—until one small article, only a few paragraphs in length, riveted his attention.

A sailor from White Bear Lake had been sighted in his homemade ten-foot sailboat about 400 miles south of Land's End, England. He was expected to reach Falmouth in only a few days.

Davis stared at the story in front of him. He had been aware of *Yankee Girl*'s departure almost two months earlier and had read that account with interest. No one had ever crossed the Atlantic single-handedly in a boat that size; Davis had only hoped that the sailor would get back home safely.

Now, it appeared, Gerry Spiess was going to make it—and set a world record.

This local story could be an exclusive for Davis.

To him, the idea of someone crossing the Atlantic alone in a homemade ten-foot boat had been inconceivable. He himself had been a merchant seaman on a 10,000-ton steel ship that had once been forced to turn around in mid-voyage because the North Atlantic had been too rough.

But here was a Minnesota schoolteacher who had designed and built his own little wooden yacht in his garage, had crossed those same seas, and was now nearing England.

As far as Davis, an Englishman, was concerned, the story had everything. If Spiess succeeded, he would be a hero not only in the States but in England as well.

He shoved back his chair and headed for the office of his assignment editor, Tom Wayne. After some discussion, Wayne agreed that the story was perfect for TV.

There could be problems in covering it, though. Davis would have to get final approval immediately in order to fly to England on time. He would have to shuffle his other assignments—and reschedule the vacation he'd planned to take with his wife beginning on the following day. And, of course, he'd have to convince someone that the project was worth the thousands of dollars it would cost the station.

That someone was Stanley S. Hubbard, KSTP's president and general manager. Hubbard was a slim, wiry man in his forties who belonged to a yacht club, owned several boats, and loved sailing. Davis suspected that Hubbard would go for the story.

But first he had some homework to do—and time was slipping by.

Davis knew that Sally Spiess, Gerry's wife, would probably be leaving for England almost immediately, and he wanted to talk with her before then. He decided to risk catching her at home.

Glancing occasionally at the address he'd written on a piece of note paper, Davis drove out to White Bear Lake. But when he arrived at the Spiess's house and knocked on the door, no one answered. So he walked around the neighborhood, trying to find someone who knew where Sally was.

Finally he spoke with a woman who thought she could get Sally's work number—but she'd have to call him back.

Davis left her his number and returned to KSTP, resigned to the fact that he'd have to try to contact Sally later in the evening.

To his surprise, a man soon called him with the number he needed.

Davis didn't waste any time.

"Sally Spiess here," said the voice on the other end of the line.

"Mrs. Spiess, this is Jason Davis, KSTP. I understand that your husband, Gerry, is going to make it."

"Yes!" she responded enthusiastically. Then she paused. How had this reporter managed to find her? She hadn't given out her business number to anyone from the local media.

But Gerry's crossing *was* news—and it was time for the rest of the world to hear about it. Sally agreed to let Davis interview her early the next morning, before she left for England.

At the end of their conversation, he had one final question.

"Has anyone from WCCO-TV called you?"

He needed to know whether KSTP's rival of long standing was also on to his story.

"No," Sally said.

Davis was pleased.

"I'll come by in the morning and shoot some material," he told her. "I'd appreciate it if you could show me any pictures you have of Gerry and the boat."

By 7 A.M. on Friday, July 20, Davis was back in White Bear Lake.

"I'm taking a plane at noon," Sally said, smiling as she indicated the luggage standing near the door.

As they talked, she showed him photographs, charts, and news clippings—and answered the countless questions Davis had prepared.

Why was Gerry doing this? Had he ever attempted such a voyage before? Was she worried? Would she get to England in time for his arrival?

Following the interview, the KSTP film crew shot footage of the exterior of the Spiess home and the surrounding neighborhood.

It would all look good on the 10:00 news that night.

But Davis wasn't quite satisfied. He wanted to add a dramatic touch, something that would drive home what he felt by now was a "thumping good, fundamental news story." So he drove to the shore of White Bear Lake—the same lake on which Gerry had tested his little *Yankee Girl*. There he found a ten-foot dinghy. Just what he needed.

Shoving off as the cameras rolled, Davis stood up in the boat, which bobbed alarmingly under his weight.

"This," he said, holding out his arms, "is the length of the boat in which Gerry Spiess is attempting to cross the Atlantic."

Now *that* was the way to end a thumping good story.

When Davis returned to the KSTP building, he met Tom Wayne in the cafeteria. He was surprised to learn that Wayne had already talked with Stanley Hubbard about the story.

"I asked him when we were going to England," Wayne informed Davis. "I didn't know that you hadn't told him yet."

"What did he say?" Davis asked eagerly.

"He wanted to know why we wanted to go—and when I explained, he gave me instructions to find out how much it would cost."

"That's a good sign," Davis said.

Davis noticed that Hubbard was also having his lunch in the cafeteria. Pulling out the news clipping Sally had given him that morning, he made his way between the tables toward the man who would make the final decision.

"Here's the story on the White Bear Lake sailor," Davis said, handing Hubbard the clipping.

"Do you think we should go?" Hubbard asked as he scanned the story.

"Yes," Davis answered, trying to control his enthusiasm.

Hubbard paused for a moment. Then he looked up at Davis.

"Okay. Go."

Davis caught his breath. The story was his.

But that meant that he'd have to be in England, 5,000 miles away, by Sunday—and it was already Friday afternoon.

My decision to head straight for England had been a good one. For the most part, the 18 days which followed had been fair and sunny. The breezes had been variable but favorable, allowing me to either reach or run.

I had been sailing around the clock and getting bolder by the minute. On some nights I'd even slept with the spinnaker up, a practice that would have alarmed the most experienced sailor. The 180-square-foot sail—*Yankee Girl*'s largest—had never given me any problems, but I had kept a close eye on the weather just in case.

My little girl and I were making astonishing progress, covering between 78 and 81 nautical miles per day. On July 15, we had set a record: 84 miles in 24 hours, our longest run of the voyage.

Our speed was exhilarating and did wonders for my spirits.

After the terrors of the storm, the past several days had seemed perfect by comparison—balmy and sweet. It almost felt as if we were riding a tradewind passage. By mid-morning the sun was usually warm, but not burning, and I'd raise my umbrella and delve into my stockpile of reading materials. I had so little work to do that I could spend hours simply relaxing.

I took pleasure in everything—*Yankee Girl*'s drive toward England, the billow of the red sail above me, the blue sky, the steady breeze, the open horizons. While the sea had formerly been an adversary, it had now become my friend. It slipped by with a pleasant gurgle, mile after mile.

I especially enjoyed the simple act of eating. Food was no longer something I stuffed into myself to keep my weight and strength up; I had fun with it. On one beautiful Saturday night, under the brilliant light of a full moon, I got out my cooking pot, put a little oil in the bottom, lighted the propane, and popped a batch of popcorn. Then I happily devoured it all, relishing my "night out."

The weather had put me at ease. I often went to sleep with my radio on, luxuriating in *Yankee Girl*'s rhythmic motion as I drowsed to the voices of the BBC or Radio Madrid. For once I didn't have to worry about whether my provisions would hold out, or my batteries would corrode, or my gasoline supply would be sufficient—or any of the other concerns that had nagged at me earlier.

Occasionally I had "visitors." Sea birds—shearwaters and terns and storm petrels—would circle the air above the boat; some would even try to land on the mast. Schools of fish would flash and gleam through the water around us. But my favorites were the porpoises, those marvelous, intelligent creatures with the perpetual grins.

One morning I was awakened by a chorus of piercing, high-pitched squeals. As I looked out over the transom, I saw dozens of porpoises diving and weaving around and under the boat. It almost seemed as if they had been waiting for me to climb out of bed and say hello. I could hear them talking to one another, and I tried to communicate with them by whistling. I even brought my radio up to see if they would find it interesting.

They were as curious about me as I was about them. One mother brought her baby up to look at me, gently nudging it away when it passed some invisible boundary she'd drawn. From time to time, others would swim near—some almost close enough to touch. But most of them glided ahead of the boat, somersaulting through the air.

Usually, though, I was very much alone. For weeks my life and my thoughts had been intertwined with *Yankee Girl* and the endless ocean. I had developed great affection for them both, but I had been at sea too long: I was eager to return to my family and friends.

If all went well, I would see them soon. It was now Thursday, July 19—49 days into my voyage. I would be in England shortly, perhaps by Sunday, July 22.

The only thing that had disturbed my 18-day idyll had been the fact that I'd been unable to contact anyone since June 30. And even this worry had been taken care of. Only the day before I'd been able to reach a ship and send a message home.

I had been standing on the cabin top, looking around, when I noticed masts on the horizon. Although previous attempts at calling ships in the distance had been unsuccessful, I decided to try once more.

An answer came back within moments.

"This is the *Potomac*, a freighter nine days out of Philadelphia and bound for Rotterdam."

There was a pause.

"We can't figure this out," the voice went on. "We can receive you fine, but we can't see you."

"I've got a big red spinnaker up," I responded, "but you won't see me because I'm below your horizon. I'm in a ten-foot boat headed for Falmouth out of Virginia."

"How long have you been at sea?" asked the voice incredulously.

"Forty-nine days. I'm making good progress. Actually, my family isn't expecting me so soon. It's important that I get a message to them because they haven't heard from me in quite a while. Can you help?"

"No problem. What can we do for you?"

"Just get a message back, if you will. That will really make my day."

I gave them my message, and after that we lapsed into a long, satisfying conversation. Human contact! It meant more to me now than it ever had.

When they had pulled out of range, a number of questions began to gnaw at me. I was confident that the *Potomac* would relay my message to the Coast Guard Station in Virginia, but I couldn't be sure what would happen next. Would the receiving officer get it right? Would Sally call in to the Coast Guard soon enough to get my message and change her plans? What if she didn't arrive in England until the end of July—the time we'd originally agreed on?

There were other unknowns as well. I wasn't sure what—if anything—would happen when I finally reached Falmouth. To begin with, I had only about $23 in my wallet. If Sally wasn't there to meet me, my lack of funds would quickly become embarrassing. I was dog-tired; I needed a place to rest, a place to stretch out. From the looks of things, I wouldn't even be able to afford a hotel room.

And what would I do with *Yankee Girl*? How could I possibly meet the costs involved in bringing her home—the dockage, boatyard, crating, trucking, and shipping? They would add up to almost as much as I'd invested in building her.

Suddenly I felt strangely melancholy. In some ways, these past seven weeks had been the most miserable of my life. But during them I had accomplished a long-cherished goal. My dream was coming true.

Still, I was saddened. For there was really only one sensible thing to do with *Yankee Girl* once I reached England.

I would have to sell her for whatever she would bring.

XII

Surprise!

"Behold, now, another
providence of God.
A ship comes into the harbor."
William Bradford

As the transatlantic jet began its descent toward London's Heathrow Airport, Jason Davis glanced repeatedly at his watch. They were running late. A charter aircraft was supposed to be waiting to carry him and photographer Bill Juntunen to Falmouth; Davis hoped that it would still be there when they landed.

It was Sunday, July 22, 1979.

Davis tried to relax, but it was difficult. As far as he could tell, he had an exclusive on his hands. None of the U.S. networks was planning to cover the story about the Minnesota sailor, and neither was the BBC.

A representative from British Airways greeted them as they deplaned.

"Mr. Davis of KSTP?" she asked politely.

Davis nodded, and he and Juntunen were ushered immediately to a twin-engined aircraft.

Moments later they were taxiing to the runway.

"You're two hours late," the pilot said. "Next time I suggest you gentlemen fly into the other airport."

"Why?" Davis asked.

"So you won't have to pay penalties for your charter to land here," the pilot explained. "And, because you're late, there's another penalty as well."

"What does it all add up to?" Davis asked, not really wanting to know. As the reporter behind the coverage, he would be held responsible for any expenses that were considered unusual or out of line.

"The penalty for being late is $500," the pilot said.

Davis was shocked. Five hundred dollars! How much was this project going to cost?

He pushed the question out of his mind. Right now he had more important things to think about—like whether he would get to Falmouth on time. He wanted to be there when Gerry Spiess stepped out of his tiny boat. That would be a historic event, and he wanted to witness it—and get it down on film.

An hour later they landed at the airport near Falmouth. Davis and Juntunen rented a small car and drove hard over the winding English coastal roads. When they arrived in the port city late that afternoon, they headed immediately for the Greenbank Hotel, where Davis knew Sally was staying.

He saw her as soon as he walked into the lobby.

"Gerry's still out there," Sally informed him. "But there's something else you should know." She turned and pointed.

The room was full of people.

"Reporters and photographers," Sally said. "Some of these fellows have been sleeping on the sofas for three days. There isn't a vacant room in the hotel."

Davis felt his spirits sinking. His exclusive had turned into a major media event. He didn't relish the idea of traveling 5,000 miles only to be scooped by the British press.

Later he discovered that his competition had already chartered all of the best boats, including the Yacht Club's launch. Davis's only hope was the *Link*, Falmouth's pilot boat.

When Davis learned that some of the London press had already reserved the *Link* and invited Sally and Gerry's parents on board as guests, he asked if he and Juntunen could go along.

The British reporters conferred among themselves for a few moments. The Americans wouldn't be competing with them directly, so their presence wouldn't be a problem; still. . . .

Davis awaited their verdict anxiously. Finally he was told that he and Juntunen would be welcome aboard the *Link*—*if* they each agreed to pay two shares of the cost.

Gritting his teeth, Davis accepted.

Thoughout that evening and the next day, everyone played a waiting game. Somewhere in the rough seas off the coast of England, the lone Minnesota sailor was making his way toward Falmouth. But the weather wasn't good—and the reports of his progress were few and far between.

Tuesday, July 24, dawned gray and rainy as more reporters from both British and American networks and newspapers streamed into Falmouth. They scrambled about, trying to find boats, and it became clear that a frenzied competition was on.

When the *Link* shoved off at about 9:45 A.M., visibility was down to 150 yards.

"This is a waste of time," one veteran English newsman said. "We'll never find him in this soup."

Sally stood at the rail, her face grim. Though the British Coast Guard had repeatedly tried to call Gerry, no one had been able to reach him for several hours.

He was out there *somewhere*—that much she knew. But where?

The weather began turning foul as I neared the English coast. Another worry to add to my list. This was a critical point in my journey, and success—or failure—could hinge on the next few hours.

As I approached the British Isles, the current would divide, and I would have to be careful not to be swept along in the wrong direction. If I sailed too far north, I could end up in Ireland; too far south, and I might find myself in the treacherous Bay of Biscay or on the shores of France.

I knew that my small, low-speed sailboat didn't have the power to fight against both adverse winds and currents.

I was also low on gasoline.

On the previous day I'd been able to contact a ship called the *Manchester Concept* and confirm that I was about 115 miles from Land's End, the southwesternmost tip of England. According to my charts, this was a heavily trafficked area. In fact, there were more freighters, tankers, liners, and trawlers steaming around this part of the ocean than anywhere else in the world.

It was not a good time for my visibility and maneuverability to be as limited as they were. I was also far more fatigued than I should have been on entering these dangerous waters.

All I could do was to sail as fast as possible on a heading of 60 degrees magnetic. If I steered straight and wasn't carried astray by currents, this course would bring me to Wolf Rock—or so I believed. I hadn't been able to take a proper sight this morning because of the overcast sky, and I was relying on a combination of instincts and dead reckoning.

As the day wore on, the wind swung around to the west, and I set both jibs to scud along at top hull speed. Sailing under these conditions was both exhilarating and frightening; I enjoyed zipping along at four knots, but I didn't like not knowing how close we were to the rocky cliffs of the Scilly Isles.

Mist and fog shrouded the sea. As patches lifted or cleared, I sighted ship after ship, dark strangers steaming fast for ports unknown. Frequently I tried calling them, but I never received a response. It was very frustrating. I was literally surrounded by ships, any of which could have confirmed my position, but no one bothered to answer my general radio call.

By late afternoon I was seriously concerned about my position. I had been running steadily under twin jibs with a brisk wind and making good progress, but I still didn't know where I was. Was I getting closer to—or farther from—my destination? I had no way of finding out.

When I sighted another ship off on the horizon, I radioed her without much hope of a reply.

Suddenly I heard words emerging through the static.

"*Yankee Girl . . . Yankee Girl . . .*"

They were faint and faraway, but they were there.

Desperately afraid of losing even that tenuous contact, I called again and again.

Then, like a whisper, the voice came back to me.

"This is Land's End Coast Guard."

I was overjoyed. I was talking to someone on *land!*

"Can you give me a bearing?" I inquired, praying that our radio link would hold up.

"Sorry, *Yankee Girl*, we don't have the equipment to do that. What is your estimated position?"

"I'm about 25 miles southwest of Land's End, course 60 degrees magnetic. Over."

Even with the volume turned up full, I couldn't understand their static-riddled reply.

Finally I gave up.

"Thank you, Land's End, out," I said. I would try later, when I drew closer to them.

I turned my attention to my radio direction finder. The night before I had made several unsuccessful attempts to pick up one of the radio beacons that might have helped me pinpoint my position. Today my luck was no better; I'd just have to wait for darkness. Then, if I could see only one recognizable light, I'd know whether we were sailing into danger.

Visibility during the night was further reduced by rain squalls, and this made me more nervous than ever. The shipping traffic had increased, and at one time I counted eight ships heading in different directions around me. Simply staying out of their way was enough to keep me busy.

I was having difficulty seeing the white, red, and green lights of these speeding leviathans through the rain and mist, and I could imagine how hard it was for them to see me. So I made every attempt to make myself noticeable. I hoisted my strobe light to the masthead, rigged the radar reflector, and occasionally shined my flashlight on the sails. I knew, though, that these precautions wouldn't help much if a ship came straight at me.

Sometimes I smelled passing ships even when I couldn't see them. The reek of diesel fumes and grease or the aromas of food and coffee would waft toward me over the water, startling me. Then I would speculate on their cargoes and destinations of these ghostly vessels and hope that our paths wouldn't cross in the fog.

At about 10 P.M. I reduced sail to the main only. This slowed *Yankee Girl* down and gave me slightly better visibility and control. Afterward I stayed on deck, looking for lights of any kind.

Finally, at around midnight, I saw a flashing light off to the north.

"This might be it, Ger," my imaginary friend exclaimed.

"Keep your fingers crossed," I answered.

Controlling my impatience, I reached into my navigation box and carefully removed my only working watch from its plastic bag. I'd kept it there for weeks to protect it. The one I'd been wearing when I left Virginia had long since stopped, and I couldn't afford to lose this one too.

I timed the light's period at 30 seconds.

But when I consulted my light lists, there was no mention of a 30-second light.

Something had gone wrong. I had been carried too far north.

With my arm crooked around the mast, I stood in the misty

rain for what seemed like hours, staring at that blinking light. Slowly the simple facts began to penetrate my sleep-dazed brain.

What I was seeing wasn't a 30-second light after all. Instead it was a beacon flashing white at the end of 15 seconds, then red after 15 more seconds, and then white again. The red was obscured by the weather conditions.

I examined my light lists once more.

I was looking at the light on Wolf Rock.

We had made a perfect landfall!

I sailed directly toward it—and saw the red flash just before another squall moved in to obliterate it.

Now I estimated my distance to be about 10 to 14 miles off the coast. I headed for Lizard Point, where I would find another beacon to guide me safely to Falmouth.

By this time fatigue and poor visibility were combining to confuse me. I was finding it more and more difficult to interpret the myriad lights of the ships around me and determine their distance, course, and speed. As I tried to stay clear of these other ships, I was continually thrown off my heading, often coming to a full stop with the mainsail luffing.

I knew that the Lizard Light flashed three seconds on and three seconds off, and I knew where to look for it, but I only saw it once. By the time I reached for my hand bearing compass it had disappeared again in the rain.

My only choice at this point was to maintain a more easterly direction and wait for daylight, when I should be able to see the cliffs.

Dawn broke at about 4 A.M., bringing with it a pea-soup fog that limited visibility to a hazardous 50 yards. I was now in the midst of the east-west shipping lane, and I had to turn my head every few seconds to listen and smell for ships.

Finally I dropped the mainsail and yanked the Evinrude to life. I would have to risk using up the rest of my gasoline; I desperately needed the maneuverability that my motor would give me. With the engine at full throttle and a hull speed of four knots, I'd at least have a chance to scoot away if anything loomed out of the fog toward me.

"I don't like this part, Ger," my friend complained.

"Me neither," I replied.

I felt as if some shadowy force had played a terrible trick on me. I had journeyed 3,800 miles across the Atlantic only to encounter a deadly fog that impaired my visibility when I needed it the most.

I began imagining that ships were creeping up on me from all directions. I could almost see the black walls of steel slicing out of the greenish-white fog bank.

If a ship did hit *Yankee Girl,* my little plywood boat would be crushed in an instant.

The strong tidal currents along the coast were also making me uneasy. They could easily carry a vessel astray and toss it up against the craggy, treacherous Cornwall coastline. Many sailors had lost their lives on those surf-pounded rocks.

I had altered my course to 90 degrees so I wouldn't come up in the windward side of the Lizard and have it as my lee shore. But I still didn't know how far away the rocks were.

Suddenly I raised my head and listened.

Had I heard a sound?

I turned off my motor and waited.

It had come from a long way off, deep-throated and urgent.

There it was again: the booming drone of the Lizard's foghorn! A long blast followed by a short one—Morse code for the letter N.

At last I knew exactly where I was. The Lizard's horn was bearing due north; that meant that I'd been pushed eastward by the current.

I started up the engine again and headed at top speed directly toward the Lizard. After ten minutes I shut down the motor, listened, and took a new bearing. Then I pulled on the Evinrude's starting cord and motored some more. I kept repeating this procedure until the horn was loud enough for me to hear even with the engine running.

I was now so close to that mammoth horn that I could almost feel its vibrations in the moisture-laden air. But foghorns can play tricks, changing their range and direction with atmospheric conditions and luring unsuspecting sailors into the very dangers they warn against. So, to be on the safe side, I turned east once more.

At about 9 A.M. a miracle occurred: the fog lifted.

And there, spread out before me like a vision, were the jagged cliffs of Cornwall.

The scene literally took my breath away.

Rising above the cliffs was the sparkling white Lizard Point light. Just beyond lay amber fields, outlined neatly by foliage-covered stone walls. It was a fairyland, a paradise.

A faint zephyr drifted toward me, bearing the scent of new-mown hay.

I inhaled that intoxicating fragrance again and again. I couldn't get enough of it. After weeks of breathing sea air, the smell of something green and living was wonderful to me. I wanted to fill my lungs with it, to take it into every pore of my body.

In spite of everything, I thought, *I'm a land animal. I love the sea, but I belong to the land.*

Slowly I forced myself back to reality and began making preparations to enter port. I could have stared at Cornwall forever, but I still had another 12 miles to go before reaching Falmouth.

I only hoped that they would go quickly. I was eager for my voyage to be over.

No longer worried about my fresh water supply, I washed my face and hands until they squeaked. Then I crawled forward until I found the plastic bag containing my clean white sweater and slacks. I had stowed them there after leaving Virginia, wanting to save them for this very special occasion. After I changed my clothes, I brushed my teeth and combed my hair and beard.

"You *look* clean," my friend commented, "but I wouldn't want to be downwind of you."

I had one more job left to do. I took out my British ensign

and my American flag and hoisted them both according to flag etiquette, with the host country's emblem at the mast-head.

I was puttering around below, tidying up the cabin, when I was startled by the sound of a klaxon.

I glanced up.

A boat was coming down the coast at full speed, and it was heading directly for me.

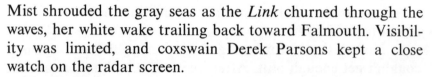

Mist shrouded the gray seas as the *Link* churned through the waves, her white wake trailing back toward Falmouth. Visibil-ity was limited, and coxswain Derek Parsons kept a close watch on the radar screen.

The mood in the pilot house was glum. Most of the report-ers stood at the windows, scanning the waters for any sign of *Yankee Girl.*

The radio crackled with messages, but the facts were not encouraging: in this fog, and without a definite bearing, it would be difficult if not impossible to find the little yacht.

Parsons knew this part of the ocean well, however. And he also knew that an experienced sailor like Spiess would follow the safest course possible in these conditions.

He leaned over his chart and thought aloud.

"If I were Gerry, I'd probably stay well east of the Lizard to avoid the tidal rips and a possible lee shore."

Then, reaching for a pencil, he drew a rectangular box on the chart.

"We should find him somewhere in this area," Parsons said, satisfied.

One British newsman looked over his shoulder at Parsons and turned back to a colleague, shaking his head.

"Despite what he says, we'd best plan on coming out again tomorrow. No telling where the American is now—or even if he made it through this beastly weather."

His companion nodded in agreement.

Out on the bow, with his coat collar turned up against the raw weather, Jason Davis was interviewing Sally.

"Do you think we'll be able to find him?" he asked.

"Of course we will," Sally replied confidently. "It's just a matter of *when*."

Davis was about to ask another question when one of the London reporters came racing out of the wheelhouse.

"Is that it?" the reporter shouted, pointing off to starboard.

"Where?" Sally exclaimed.

"That little blue thing over there. . . ."

Sally leaped to the rail excitedly.

She stared out into the mist—and then she saw it.

"YES!" she cried. "Yes, that's *Yankee Girl!*"

Davis hurried after her, holding up the microphone as photographer Bill Juntunen continued to film.

"Sally," he began, "how do you feel?"

But Sally didn't hear his question. She was no longer conscious of Davis, or the cameraman, or anyone else. She strained forward over the rail, staring at the horizon, waiting for the tiny boat to emerge from the mist once more.

"There he is!" she shouted. "Over there!"

Parsons now took a visual heading, and the *Link* bore down on *Yankee Girl*.

"But where's Gerry?" someone asked.

The pilot boat's klaxon sounded.

"Ahoy, *Yankee Girl!*" Sally yelled across the diminishing distance.

By this time the reporters were jostling one another for a place along the rail. They all saw *Yankee Girl*'s startled skipper pop up through the hatch of his boat.

"I can see his head," Davis said.

"He's got a beard," Sally noted incredulously.

"You swore he wouldn't have."

"Well, I'll bet he won't have it when he gets cleaned up!"

In moments the *Link* was alongside *Yankee Girl.*
The little yacht bobbed like a cork in the larger boat's
wake.

I had never been so surprised in my life.

When I looked up to see the pilot boat racing toward me
over the water, all I could think about was getting out of her
way.

And then I saw Sally.

After that everything happened very quickly.

The pilot boat was crammed full of people—Sally, my parents, newspaper and TV reporters, photographers, camera-
men, crew members. Everyone was smiling and shouting at
once, waving at me and calling out questions.

"What was the most dangerous part of your trip?"

"Did you run out of food or water?"

"Were you menaced by sharks or whales?"

It was sheer pandemonium. After weeks of longing desperately for someone to talk to, I was speechless.

All during this barrage of questions, the only people I really
noticed were Sally and my parents.

"Gerry . . . Gerry!" my dad kept yelling.

"Did you get any sleep last night?" Sally wanted to know.

"Gerry, you look so *good*!" my mother exclaimed.

I was choking back tears.

Finally one voice boomed out over the others.

"What do you have to say after 54 days alone at sea?"
came the question.

There was a hush as everyone waited for my answer. I saw
pencils poised and microphones extended to capture my first
words.

"Well, I made it," I said lamely.

It wasn't the profound statement they'd all been expecting,

but it was the best I could come up with in my dazed state.

And it wasn't an absolutely truthful answer, either. I hadn't *quite* made it—not yet. I was still 12 miles out of Falmouth. Since my top speed was only about four knots and I would be bucking an ebb tide the whole way, I had to get going.

We all waved a temporary good-bye and I started my little motor again. The pilot boat rapidly overtook me, and its wake rocked *Yankee Girl* from side to side nearly down to her gunwales. The *Link*'s speed, I suspected, was due to the urging of the reporters on board, who were eager to file their stories.

I was glad to be alone again. I needed time to think about what had just happened.

But soon another boat bearing a full contingent of reporters and photographers from CBS, ABC, and other networks pulled up alongside. More questions. More pictures. I talked with them as I motored along.

Where were all of these media people coming from? And how had they found out about me?

When they had their story, they roared off toward Falmouth—and another powerboat zoomed up. It, too, was packed with reporters and photographers.

Never before had I faced so many cameras and microphones. For a moment, I wondered if I was dreaming.

I heard a noise overhead. Two helicopters from the Royal Navy were circling above me, their crew members leaning precariously out the doorways to wave. They were followed by several small airplanes, also full of waving, smiling, picture-taking people.

I waved back, mystified.

Sooner or later, I thought, this would have to stop.

But I was wrong. Now several large sailboats motored toward me, their crews gesturing and shouting across the water.

"Well done!"

"Good show!"

One of them drew close enough for me to ask advice on the

best way into Falmouth. I was told to stay as near to the coast as possible to avoid the worst of the ebb tide.

I had the engine turned up full, and *Yankee Girl* was making her best speed, but even so it was several hours before I sighted the entrance to the harbor. Meanwhile more traffic came out to greet me.

It was clear that I wasn't going to have a minute to myself.

I was beginning to worry about all of the boats crowding around me. Sometimes there would be one boat in front of me, another nearly alongside, and a third behind me when yet another would come out of nowhere and dart into the space between us. Everyone was shouting congratulations and questions. Several skippers offered me beers—which I declined— and one man handed me a Cornish flag.

As I neared the harbor, I couldn't believe my eyes.

An entire flotilla of boats was streaming toward me. There were dozens of cruisers, sailboats, open launches, and even small inflatables with outboard motors—each one racing through the water, eager to get to me first.

Before I knew what was happening, I was completely surrounded. A mass collision seemed imminent. I had to keep motoring along at the same speed in a straight line simply to avoid being run over.

With some good-natured shouting and gesturing, my ragtag escort soon formed itself into a gigantic nautical parade.

Whe-e-e-e-oh!

That was a Navy cruiser blowing its whistle in salute. The other vessels echoed the greeting, adding to the general cacophony with their own horns, whistles, and bells. Everywhere people were applauding and cheering.

When we entered the harbor, it almost seemed as if the city of Falmouth rose up to welcome me.

Nestled at the foot of castle-crowned hills, it was beautiful.

For a moment I forgot about the shouting, waving people around me and stared at my destination, the point at which my journey would finally end.

I was sailing into a haven that had hosted centuries of privateers, men-of-war, Chinese tea and Australian wool clippers, and many of the single-handers I had read about during my years of planning and dreaming.

I was glad I had chosen this harbor as my goal.

With a jolt, I was drawn back into the present.

There were people everywhere. Crowds lined the piers, quays, and hillside roads leading to Pendennis Castle. Thousands of people, all cheering and clapping.

I *had* to be dreaming. What had happened to my vision of a quiet docking?

The situation was fast becoming hazardous. Boats were bumping into one another wherever I looked. I was beginning to wonder what to do next when I saw the Harbour Master's boat shouldering its way toward me.

"Welcome to Falmouth, sir, and congratulations," the Harbour Master said warmly. "Please follow us."

He maneuvered his vessel until it was directly in front of *Yankee Girl*'s bow and cleared a path for us through the water.

As I neared the mooring that had been set aside for me—another surprise—the clamor intensified. Those people who weren't cheering were blowing horns, whistles, and other noisemakers.

When I stepped out of *Yankee Girl*, I was led like a sleepwalker to the Customs Launch, where the entry paperwork was awaiting my signature. Meanwhile my little boat was towed away by the Harbour Master's men for safekeeping. If they hadn't arranged to do this, I later learned, the tourists might have stripped her bare for souvenirs.

After signing the entry papers, I was taken by launch to the steps of the Falmouth Yacht Club for a formal welcome. Dad and Mother and Sally were there, along with Falmouth's Mayor, Olive White, and other local dignitaries. Behind them stood crowds of news people, tourists, and what seemed like the entire population of Falmouth.

Someone handed me a glass of champagne, and the Mayor stepped forward, smiling warmly.

"We're proud to welcome you to Falmouth," she said, "a port that has played host to so many other courageous seamen. May your stay in Cornwall be a pleasant and restful one."

The crowd cheered as photographers jostled one another and reporters shouted question after question. Everyone was pushing and shoving everyone else. For a moment, as I looked at the mass of people surging toward me, I was afraid I'd find myself back in the water again.

Through the crush, I could see one cameraman crawling between people's legs on his hands and knees. It was Bill Juntunen, determined to get his film.

On top of the stress of my voyage, this reception was almost too much. Suddenly I was aware that my legs felt like rubber bands and the earth seemed to be tilting crazily back and forth.

"Are you okay, Ger?" Sally asked. "Why don't you put your arm around my shoulder and lean on me?"

I held her tightly.

It took us nearly twenty minutes to wind our way to the Greenbank Hotel, only half a block away. People pressed forward to shake my hand, congratulate me, or squeeze my arm. Several elderly ladies planted motherly kisses on my cheek.

At the hotel, Sally and I were guided directly through the lobby and up the stairs to our large, cheery room overlooking the harbor.

"Rest for a few moments," someone called out encouragingly.

A few moments? I was planning on a longer rest than that. A few *weeks* seemed more like it.

I closed the door behind us.

"Now," I sighed, "we can relax."

"Not quite yet, I'm afraid," Sally replied, arching an eyebrow. "There's a press conference being set up on the balcony—and another reception in the lobby."

My face fell.

"Ger, we *have* to go down," she said gently. "Some of these people have been waiting for three days to see you."

"How did they know I was coming?" I asked. I still found it hard to believe that so many reporters and photographers had come to Falmouth just to see me.

"The Coast Guard in Portsmouth contacted the Associated Press right after you talked to the *Bilderdyk.* You've been in the newspapers ever since."

"Don't I even have time for a bath?" I pleaded desperately.

"You've waited two months; another hour or so won't make that much difference."

Reluctantly I staggered back down the stairs.

Another glass of champagne was pressed into my hand as we were led to our seats in the glare of the television lights.

The questions started coming almost immediately.

"Did you have any bad moments?"

"How were you able to cope with the loneliness?"

"Were you frightened?"

"Did you ever feel like giving up?"

In spite of my fatigue, I did my best to answer each question. My exhaustion must have been apparent, though, because at last a very proper British journalist stood up and signaled for silence.

"I think Mr. Spiess deserves a rest and a slap-up meal," he said.

The others rose to their feet and applauded as we made our way to the Hotel's elegant dining room.

And there was the final surprise of the day: a long banquet table covered with pressed white linen, neatly arranged napkins, silver, china, and crystal. Sally, my parents, and I were seated at the head, with Mayor White, other Falmouth dignitaries, and about a dozen London reporters flanking us.

"Would you like some water, Mr. Spiess?" a waitress asked politely.

I nodded. It felt odd to have people waiting on me.

"Would you rather have peas or carrots?" another asked.

"I'll have some of each, please," I heard myself saying.

"Creamed or fried potatoes?"

"Both, please."

Secretly I wished that someone would put everything on the table in front of me and be done with it. After weeks of eating out of cans, I was starved for fresh food. And it was wonderful to sit upright without having to brace myself. I'd almost forgotten how good it felt to sit still. I could tell that I was in for a lengthy, luxurious period of rediscovering life's little pleasures.

As the crowning touch, we had steak for our main course. Barely able to control my impatience, I waited to start eating until everyone had been served. I was tempted to sneak a bite, but I managed to restrain myself.

I couldn't believe how marvelous my first bite of real meat tasted. It paled, however, beside the rolls and butter. Fresh bread! Real creamery butter! I gobbled roll after roll, hoping no one would notice.

What a feast!

The evening passed in a blur of questions, congratulations, phone calls, and telegrams from around the world. It wasn't until 2 A.M. that Sally and I were able to break away and trudge upstairs to our room.

"Now for that bath," I said.

"You've earned it," she answered, grinning.

I peeled my clothes away from my skin as Sally filled the oversized pink tub with steaming water and sprinkled it with bubble bath. When she was finished, she turned to look at me.

"Good heavens," she gasped.

She stared in disbelief at my bruises, scaling skin, and flaming red rash.

"We'll have to get you to a doctor first thing in the morning," she said, shaking her head. "What on earth did you do to yourself out there?"

"I'll tell you later," I replied, stepping into the tub.

At first the pain was intense. I gritted my teeth and waited for my raw skin to get accustomed to the hot water. Soon I could sense the warmth radiating through me, soothing my aches.

I sighed in relief.

"You just can't imagine how great it feels to relax at last," I said.

Sally leaned over the tub and began shampooing my hair.

"The voyage is all behind you now."

"I can't believe it's over."

I reached up and took her soapy hands in mine.

"At last we're together again, Sal."

"And I'm so grateful to have you back."

She slumped down beside the tub, still holding my hands.

Somewhere in Falmouth Harbor, *Yankee Girl* was resting peacefully. Tomorrow I would have to give her a thorough checking over to see how she'd weathered our Atlantic crossing. Tonight, though, she'd have to get along without me.

"My little girl did a good job out there," I told Sally.

"You knew she would," she answered.

I closed my eyes and rested my head against the back of the tub, supremely content.

Epilogue

"The reward of a thing
well done, is to have done it."
Ralph Waldo Emerson

The early morning sunlight brightens the picture window overlooking the small park behind our house. It is here, at the kitchen table, that I love to sit and dream.

Although nearly two years have passed since I first set sail for England, the great adventure that began on that day has never really ended. It has changed my life, and will keep changing my life, forever.

I'm not building any boats at the moment, but out garage is still a "boatyard"—with *Yankee Girl* sitting inside on her trailer. As it turned out, I didn't have to sell her after all. Thanks to ABC-TV, she flew home in style on a 747.

I often go out to visit my little girl. Sometimes I spend hours in her tiny cabin, reminiscing. During the past several months I've made some minor repairs on her, and now she's as sound and seaworthy as she was before our voyage.

A number of museums have asked to put her on permanent display, so I know she'll be well taken care of when it finally comes time to retire her.

But that may be a while. I'm not ready to give her up just yet.

I never anticipated the welcome I received in England, or the tremendous interest other people have shown in my crossing, or the demands that have been placed on my time since my return. I've worked hard to keep up with a busy schedule of lectures, boat shows, and personal appearances. Whenever it becomes overwhelming, a session inside *Yankee Girl* always brings me to my senses again.

I've had a lot of fun as a result of my journey. When my boat was first put on display at Northwestern National Bank in Minneapolis, for example, a lot of people asked whether they could have some of my leftover cans of food for souvenirs. We decided instead to hold an auction and donate the money to the St. Paul Children's Hospital.

I'd come back from England with over 270 pounds of food, so there were hundreds of items to bid on. They sold for between $5 and $200 each, bringing in a total of more than $5,400 for the hospital.

This opportunity to do something for others was both unexpected and gratifying. I'd undertaken my voyage for purely personal reasons and with purely personal goals in mind: to test my ideas and to challenge myself. I had derived a great deal of satisfaction from it. The fact that others could benefit from it as well was an added bonus.

There have been other bonuses too. Perhaps it's the teacher in me that most enjoys my new occupation as lecturer. For it gives me the chance to speak my mind on something I consider terribly important.

Many of us grow up with dreams we never realize. We don't take time to live them, or we let others discourage us. We listen to the choruses of "why bother?" and "what will you gain from it?" and never experience the joys of achieving goals we set for ourselves.

I believe that everyone should have a dream and strive to reach it. People's dreams can be big or small—it doesn't matter. What matters is that a dream come true can change a person in some undefinable but vital way.

And sometimes—here's the best part—one dream will lead to another, and another, until finally the act of dreaming becomes an endless cycle, a limitless horizon as vast as the sea itself.

Editor's Note
On June 1, 1981,
Gerry Spiess and Yankee Girl
left Long Beach, California
on a five-month journey
across the Pacific Ocean.
Their destination:
Sydney, Australia,
7,800 miles away.

Appendixes and Glossary

Appendix A

The Voyage of *Yankee Girl*

Departure:
June 1, 1979
7:30 A.M., Eastern Daylight Time
Virginia Beach, Virginia
U.S.A.
Arrival:
July 24, 1979
4:30 P.M., Greenwich Mean Time
Falmouth, Cornwall
England

Elapsed time:
53 days 5 hours
Total distance:
3,287 nautical miles
3,780 statute miles
Average daily run:
60 nautical miles
Best day's run:
84 nautical miles

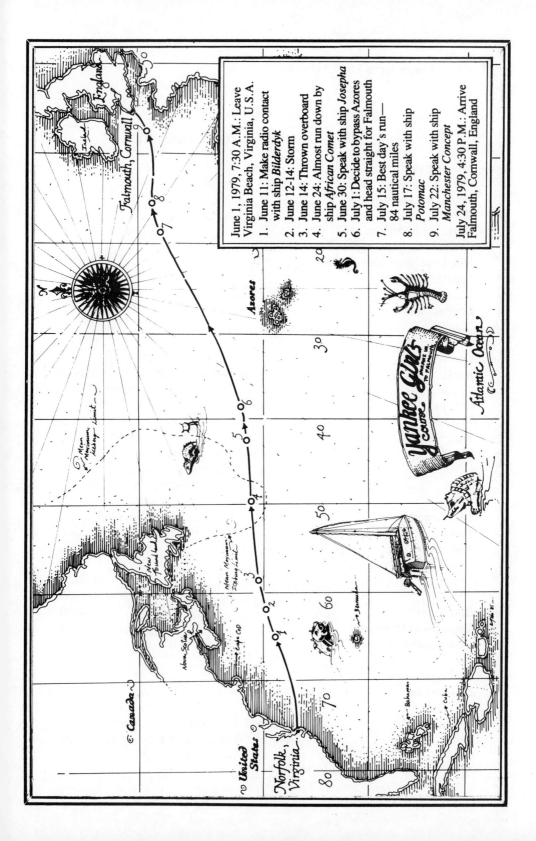

June 1, 1979, 7:30 A.M.: Leave
Virginia Beach, Virginia, U.S.A.
1. June 11: Make radio contact
   with ship *Bilderdyk*
2. June 12-14: Storm
3. June 14: Thrown overboard
4. June 24: Almost run down by
   ship *African Comet*
5. June 30: Speak with ship *Josepha*
6. July 1: Decide to bypass Azores
   and head straight for Falmouth
7. July 15: Best day's run—
   84 nautical miles
8. July 17: Speak with ship
   Potomac
9. July 22: Speak with ship
   Manchester Concept

July 24, 1979, 4:30 P.M.: Arrive
Falmouth, Cornwall, England

Appendix B

Yankee Girl: Description and Specifications

Measurements:

Overall length . . . . 10'0"
Length on the waterline . . . . 9'8"
Beam . . . . 5'6"
Draft (to bottom of skeg) . . . . 1'10"
Freeboard . . . . 1'8"
Height of mast above waterline . . . . 17'2"
Length of boom . . . . 7'6"
Weight (empty): . . . . 750 lbs.

Displacement:

Normal . . . . 1900 lbs.
At departure . . . . 2200 lbs.

Construction:

Keel . . . . 6 laminations of ¾" exterior plywood
Frames . . . . ¾" exterior plywood
Stringers . . . . Laminated clear pine
Planking . . . . ⅜" exterior plywood
Hatch and hatch cover . . . . ¾" exterior plywood
Sheathing . . . . 1 layer of 10 oz. fiberglass cloth
saturated with polyester resin
Mast . . . . Aluminum, 4½" x 3" x 14'6"
Boom . . . . Wood, 2" x 4" x 7'6"
Standing rigging . . . . Stainless steel, 1 x 19
Fastenings . . . . Cadmium-plated steel screws
Adhesives . . . . resorcinol, casein

Sails:*

Main . . . . 44 sq. ft.
Jibs, 2 . . . . 39 sq. ft. each
Spinnaker . . . . 180 sq. ft.

Theoretical hull speed: . . . . 4.02 knots

Characteristics:

Positive flotation
Self-righting
Self-rescuing
Self-steering

Motor: . . . . 4 horsepower Evinrude with 5" shaft extension
Fuel: . . . . 60 gallons of gasoline (premixed)

*All sails were made by Thurston sailmakers according to Gerry's specifications

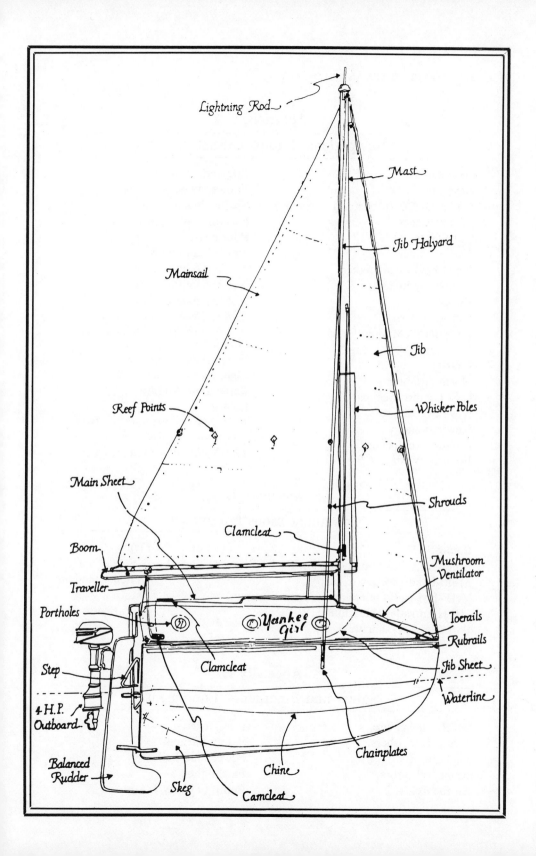

Lightning Rod

Mast

Jib Halyard

Mainsail

Jib

Reef Points

Whisker Poles

Main Sheet

Shrouds

Clamcleat

Boom

Mushroom
Ventilator

Traveller

Portholes

*Yankee
Girl*

Toerails

Rubrails

Step

Clamcleat

Jib Sheet

4 H.P.
Outboard

Waterline

Balanced
Rudder

Chainplates

Skeg

Chine

Camcleat

Appendix C

Navigational Equipment and Charts

Instruments:
Sextants, 2 (Davis)
Compasses, 3 (Davis and Airguide)
Wristwatches, 2
Calculator
Thermometer
Hand-held anemometer
Related equipment:
Dividers
Parallel rulers
Binoculars (Manon 7 x 35)
Lead line
Charts:
North Atlantic
U.S. Eastern Seaboard
Nova Scotia
Newfoundland
Azores Archipelago
Ireland, Western Coast

England, Western Coast
France, Western Coast
Spain, Western Coast
Portugal, Western Coast
Pilot charts:
North Atlantic, May
North Atlantic, June
North Atlantic, July
North Atlantic, August
Sailing directions:
Ireland and Western Coast of
   England
North Atlantic Ocean
Light list: British Isles
Radio aids: Atlantic
Books:
H.O. 249 Air Navigation Tables,
   volumes 2 and 3
The Nautical Almanac

Appendix D

Communications Equipment

Radios:
Emergency Position Indicating Radio Beacon (Narco)
Multi-band receiver (Sharp)
VHF-FM radio-telephone (Pierce-Simpson)
HF-Ham radio (Heathkit HW-7)
Portable AM/shortwave

Flags:
U.S.A.
United Kingdom
France
Q-pratique

Appendix E

Safety and Emergency Equipment

Safety equipment:
Fire extinguishers, 2
Foghorn
Radar reflectors, 2
Strobe lights, 2

Life jacket
Safety harness
Power loud hailer
Flashlights, 5
Pump (Thirsty Mate)

Emergency equipment:
Hand flares, 10
Aerial flares, 10
Dye markers, 2
Smoke bombs, 2
Signal mirror

Underwater epoxy
Mast plug
Wooden tiller hole cover
Solar still
Presaturated fiberglass patches, 2

Appendix F

Tools and Equipment

Anchors:
Bottom, 2 (Danforth 8S and 4S)
Sea, 2 (18 inch and 36 inch)
Line:
⅜" 3-strand nylon, 200 ft.
⅜" braided nylon, 100 ft.
5/16" braided Dacron, 50 ft.
¼" braided Dacron, 50 ft.
Tools:
Saw with extra blades
Brace and bits
Hand drill
Files, 2
Hatchet/hammer
Crowbar
Pop riveter
Knives, 4
Screwdrivers, 10
Wire cutters, 2
Awl
Spark plug wrench
Pliers, 6
Vise grips, 2
Chisels, 2
Allen wrenches, 1 set
Adjustable wrenches, 2
Putty knives, 2
Miscellaneous equipment:
C-clamps, 10
Silicone sealer, 2 tubes
Baster
Volt ohmmeter
Battery tester

Feeler gauges
Eyedropper
Tape measure
Adhesives
Filament tape, 4 rolls
Masking tape, 2 rolls
Electrical tape, 2 rolls
Spray lubricant, 2 cans
Solvent
Scotchbrite pads, 4
Sponges, 4
Cigarette lighters, 3
Whipping line, 4 spools
Spring clamps, 4
Adhesive tape for sails
Rubber bands
Corks
Nylon tiller hole covers, 2
5-gallon collapsible water
  containers, 4
Funnels, 3
Plastic bags
Sandpaper
Awning
Scissors, 4
Barnacle scraper
Spare parts and supplies:
Spark plugs, 20
Light bulbs, 2
AA batteries, 12
C batteries, 50
D batteries, 50
12V batteries, 6

Flints
Foghorn refills, 2
Matches, 8 books (in airtight jar)
Cable
Turnbuckles
Copper wire
Breeze clamps
Shackles
Wire clamps
Cotter pins
Shear pins
Blocks
Fairleads
Deck straps
Snaps
Cam cleats
Clam cleats
Pins
Chain
¼" plastic tubing, 10 ft.
Surgical tubing, 15 ft.
¼" shock cord, 20 ft.
Engine lubricant
Gear case lubricant
Wood
Plywood

Galley equipment:
Stove (gimbaled, propane)
Propane fuel cylinders, 24
Sterno, 10 cans
Spark igniter
Cooking pots, 2
Plates, 2
Bowls, 2
Knives, 2
Forks, 4
Spoons, 6
Beer key
Plastic tumblers, 2
Plastic cup
Measuring cup
Can openers, 2
Strainer
Spatula
Water dispensing pump
Paper towels, 8 rolls
Bar buoy drink holder

Appendix G

Provisions

Liquids:
Distilled water, 30 gallons
Condensed milk, 30 cans
Fruit juices, 88 small cans
 Apricot nectar, 24 cans
 Peach nectar, 10 cans
 Grape juice, 18 cans
 Apple juice, 36 cans
Nutrament, 12 cans
Pepsi Cola, 5 quarts
Root beer, 12 bottles
V8, 6 cans

Canned foods:
Tuna, 48 cans
Chicken, 30 cans
Vegetable beef soup, 10 cans
Chunky beef soup, 16 cans (Campbells)
Chicken ala king, 26 cans
Chili, 24 cans (Campbells)
Stew, 26 cans (Dinty Moore)
Chicken and dumplings, 20 cans
Noodles and chicken, 10 cans
Chop suey vegetables, 16 cans

Peas, 26 cans
Asparagus, 21 cans
Corn, niblets, 32 cans (Green
  Giant)
Corn, cream style, 16 cans (Green
  Giant)
Spinach, 12 cans
Tomatoes, 12 cans
Yams, 4 cans
Pears, 12 cans
Peaches, 24 cans
Pineapple, 16 cans
Apple sauce, 2 cans
Dried foods:
Beef jerky, 16 lbs. (approx. 50 lbs.
  raw)
Apples, 2 bags
Dates, 2 bags
Prunes, 1 box
Apricots, 2 bags
Coconut, 4 bags
Fresh foods:
Eggs, 5½ doz.
Apples, 15
Oranges, 40
Grapefruit, 20
Cantaloupe, 2
Lemons, 20
Bananas, 10

**Miscellaneous foods and
condiments:**
Bisquick, 1 box
Popcorn, 1 jar
Granola bars, 6 boxes
Rice, 8 pounds (Minute)
Granola, 8 pounds
Hamburger buns, 8
English muffins, 6
Vinegar
Parmesan cheese
Vegetable oil
Salt
Pepper
Sugar
Onion flakes
Onion salt
Soy sauce
Peanut butter, 2 jars
Strawberry jam, 2 jars
Tea, 24 individual bags
Related equipment:
Fishing gear
Spear
Rain catcher

Appendix H

Clothing, Toiletries, Personal Items, and Medical Supplies

Clothing:
Underwear, 35 pairs of shorts and
  T-shirts
Socks, 35 pairs
Long johns, 2 pairs
Long pants, 10 pairs
Short pants, 10 pairs
Long-sleeved shirts, 28
Short-sleeved shirts, 8
Belts, 2
Caps, 5

Wool gloves, 1 pair
Rubber gloves, 3 pairs
Tennis shoes, 3 pairs
Down jacket
Sweaters, 5
Scarf
Foul weather suits, 2
Poncho
Toiletries:
Hand lotion

Sunscreen
Sun lotion
Mirrors, 3
Nail clippers
Dental floss
Kleenex, 8 boxes
Toilet tissue, 4 rolls
Liquid hand soap, 2 bottles
Saltwater soap, 6 bars
Towels, 12
Washcloths, 10
Toothbrushes, 2
Toothpaste, 2 tubes
Combs, 2
Joy dishwashing detergent
Miscellaneous personal items:
Hand warmer
Hand warmer fuel, 3 cans
Clip-on sunglasses, 1 pair
Eyeglasses, 5 extra pairs
Clothespins
Sleeping bags, 2
Sleeping bag liners, 2
Umbrella
Sewing kit
Immunization record
Passport
Writing paper
Log book
Camera, 35mm
Pens and pencils
Insect repellent (Cutters)
Kite (Para-foil)
Snorkle
Diving mask
Medical supplies:
Band-Aids
Instant ice paks, 3
Adhesive tape
Plaster bandage
Cotton
Gauze

Surgical tape, 5 rolls
Rubbing alcohol
Ace bandages, 2
Furacin soluble dressings, 2
Sterile droppers, 2
Finger cot
Q-tips
Abdominal support
Plastic syringes, 4
Disposable needles, 9
Alcohol wipes, 12
Swab sticks, 2 pkgs.
Sterile pads, 2 doz.
*First Aid and Personal
  Safety* manual
Medications:
Vitamins
Aluminum hydroxide
Americaine topical anesthetic,
  aerosol
Desenex spray-on foot powder
Alka-Seltzer
Foille ointment
Red Cross toothache outfit
Fleet enema
Surfadil
Xylocaine
Bacitracin, 2
Diaparene, 2
Zinc oxide
Murine
Robaxin (muscle relaxant)
Donnatal
Codeine
Equagesic (pain reliever and muscle
  relaxant)
Tylenol #2
Pyribenzamine (for itching)
Dexedrine
Valium

Cortisporin Otic, 2

Bentyl (for abdominal cramps)

Lomotil

Ampicillin, 2

Demerol

Belladenal

Darvon

Gelusil

Appendix I

Books, Magazines, and Sound Equipment

Books:
The Bible
Roughing It by Mark Twain
Walden and Other Writings by Henry David Thoreau
Sailing Alone Around the World by Joshua Slocum
All Things Wise and Wonderful and *All Creatures Great and Small* by
  James Herriot
Water and Marsh Birds of the World by Oliver L. Austin
Dictionary of Fishes by Rube Allyn
Piloting, Seamanship, and Small Boat Handling by Chapman
Goode's World Atlas
Don Quixote by Miguel de Cervantes
Magazines: *Reader's Digest*, 40 issues
Sound equipment:
Tape recorder and player, Panasonic
Tapes, C-60, pre-recorded, 40

Glossary

aft toward the stern of the boat

ballast weight carried low in the hull or on the keel to give a boat stability and to balance the force of the wind on the sails

beam the width of a boat at its widest point

beam ends a boat is said to be "on its beam ends" when it is knocked over on its side

berth a bed aboard a boat; also, a boat's anchorage

bilge the lower inside areas of the hull

boom the horizontal spar that holds the lower edge of the mainsail

bow the forward end of a boat

bulkhead a vertical partition below deck

bulwarks the portion of the topsides above the level of the deck

buoy a floating object anchored in position

cam cleat a self-fastening and easily releasable cleat with teeth

capsize to overturn a boat

cast off to let go of a line; to drop all mooring lines to get a boat underway

catspaws water ruffled by a breath of wind after a calm

chainplates the strap-like metal fittings on the topsides that connect the shrouds to the hull

chine the angle formed by the bottom and topsides on flat- or vee-bottomed hulls

clam cleat a vee-shaped, self-fastening, easily releasable cleat

cleat a horned fitting to which a line is secured

coaming raised work around the cockpit or hatches that keeps water from running below

displacement a boat achieves buoyancy by *displacing* a volume of water equal in weight to the hull and its load

douse the sails to lower the sails quickly

draft the depth of water required to float a boat

drop board a vertical, removable board that, along with the hatch cover, seals the companionway; can be removed for ventilation

footwell the lowest part of the cockpit

foredeck the forward part of the deck, especially before the mast

forepeak the compartment furthest forward in the bow

forestay the wire rigging which runs from the mast to the bow

frames the ribs of a boat; the inner construction

freeboard the height of a boat's topsides from the waterline to the deck

gale-force winds on the Beaufort scale, winds ranging from 34 to 47 knots (force 8 and 9)

galley the kitchen area on a boat

garboard the lowest plank running parallel to the keel

gimbals pivoted rings that allow an object (e.g., a compass or a stove) to remain level regardless of the boat's motion

gudgeon small metal fittings secured to the stern of a small boat upon which the rudder is mounted

gunwale the upper edging of the top of a boat's sides

halyard the line used to hoist a sail

hard alee a boat is *hard alee* when the tiller is pushed to leeward in order to tack into the wind

hatch any opening in the deck which provides access below; the cover over such an opening

head the toilet area or the toilet itself on a boat (the toilet may be portable or installed)

heave to to lie almost stationary while still underway, with the bow slightly off from meeting the waves head on; a technique used during bad weather

heel to lean leeward from the force of the wind on the sails

helm the mechanism (the tiller, rudder, etc.) by which a boat is steered; to be "at the helm" is to be in control of the boat

hull the body of a boat, including the keel, the frames, and the planking

hull speed the maximum speed at which a boat can move; unless a boat has a planing hull, it cannot move faster than its hull speed regardless of how much force pushes or pulls it

jib a sail rigged forward of the mast

keel the lowest and chief structural timber in a boat, running its entire length

lash the tiller to tie down the tiller, to make it fast

leeward the direction toward which the wind is blowing; the *lee side* of a boat is the downwind side

line rope which has been put to use on board a boat

mainsail the principal sail of a boat; on a sloop like *Yankee Girl*, the mainsail is rigged from the mast and footed by the boom

mast the spar set upright to support the rigging and sails

masthead the top of the mast; the mast tip

mooring a permanent anchor, marked by a buoy

planking the wood pieces running from stem to stern that make up the outer shell of a boat's hull

point up to head the boat toward the direction of the wind

port (side) the side to the left when one is on a boat and facing forward

porthole a window in the hull to let in light and, if openable, air (also called a *port*); *Yankee Girl*'s portholes cannot be opened

rail the raised edge on a boat where the deck and the topsides join

reach to sail with the wind coming across the beam

reef the sail to reduce the sail area by partly lowering it and securing it

reef points short lengths of line attached to the sail for use when reefing the sail

rig the arrangement of mast and sails on a boat (*Yankee Girl* has a sloop rig)

rigging all the lines that secure the sails and spars on a boat

right a balanced boat *rights* itself by swinging upward after being knocked over by wind or waves

rubrail the strip of wood added externally to the planking to protect the topsides from contact with docks or pilings

rudder that by which a boat is steered; a flat piece that pivots on the sternpost (or, as on *Yankee Girl,* on the stern)

run downwind to sail with the wind coming across the stern

running rigging the sheets and halyards

scud to sail before the wind, especially before a strong wind with only enough sail to hold the boat steady

sea anchor a bucket-like apparatus that serves as a drag and holds the bow while heaving to

sextant an instrument used to determine the altitude of the sun and, from that, a boat's position at sea

sheets the lines used for adjusting the trim of the sails to the wind

shrouds the standing (fixed) rigging which extends from the mast to the sides of a boat

skeg a metal fitting on the underside of the keel that provides additional protection for the boat

slatting sail a sail that is flapping because of heavy seas and no wind

sloop a sailboat with one mast, a mainsail, and a jib

spar a general term which encompasses all of a boat's poles, including the masts and booms

spinnaker the large, almost spherical sail that flies from the masthead forward of the mast

standing rigging the shrouds and stays

starboard the side to the right when one is on a boat and facing forward

stays the (wire) lines that support the mast

steerageway the slowest forward speed of a boat that will permit steering

stem the vertical continuation of the keel at the bow

step the mast to put the mast in position on the boat

stern the after end of a boat

stow to put something in its proper place on board a boat

stringers the long, thin pieces of wood that run the length of the boat along its frame

tack to change a boat's heading by turning into the direction of the wind and falling off on the other side; on *starboard tack*, the wind comes over the boat's starboard side, while on *port tack* it comes over the boat's port side

tiller the horizontal piece extending forward from the top of the rudder by which one turns the rudder to steer the boat

toe rail the narrow strip on top of the gunwale that provides safe footing for a person on deck

topsides the sides of the boat from the waterline to the deck

transom the planking across the stern

transom knee the piece used to reinforce the stern at the point where the transom and the keel meet

traveler the device on the deck that allows close control of the mainsail's trim

trimaran a three-hulled boat

waterline the line where the water touches the hull when the boat is floating

windward the direction from which the wind is blowing; the *windward*, or "weather," *side* of a boat is the upwind side

whisker pole the spar that serves as a boom for the spinnaker

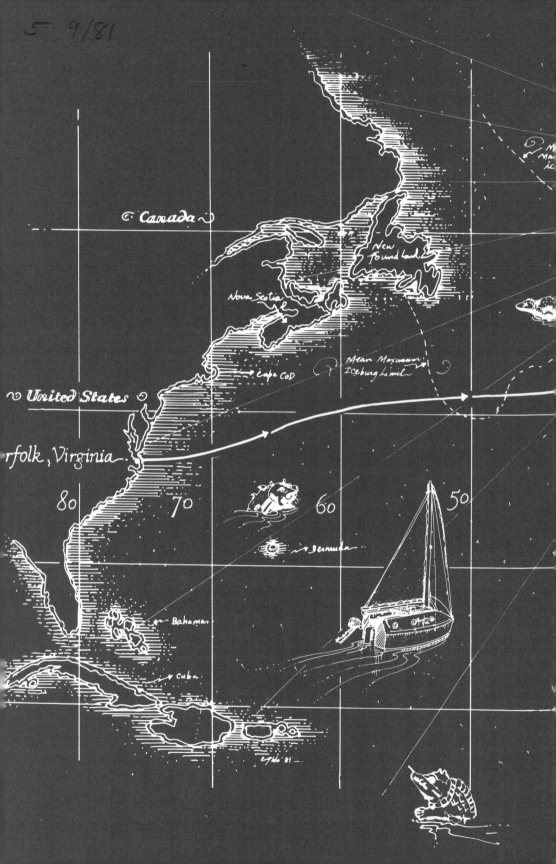